Aircraft Carrier
the majestic weapon

S0-AJR-308

Aircraft carriers

Captain D MacIntyre

Editor-in-Chief: Barrie Pitt
Art Director: Peter Dunbar

Military Consultant: Sir Basil Liddell Hart
Picture Editor: Robert Hunt

Design Assistants: Gibson/Marsh
Sandra Kingham
Cover: Denis Piper
Research Assistant: Yvonne Marsh
Cartographer: Richard Natkiel
Special Drawings: John Batchelor

Third printing: April, 1971
Fourth printing: June 1972
Printed in the United States of America

Ballantine Books Inc.
101 Fifth Avenue, New York, NY 10003

An Intext Publisher

Contents

Queen of the sea battles

Introduction by Barrie Pitt

Like so many of the weapons which played a significant part in the Second World War, the aircraft carrier was employed, in embryo form, during the First World War. Today, having lived through half a century during which developments have been largely refinements on established designs, we are apt to forget that those early attempts to produce a mobile, floating airfield were, in their halting and sometimes comic way, works of true and marvellous invention.

By dint of hard effort, great imagination, stark courage, and large slices of luck, the early aviation pioneers flew their vulnerable little kites off from, and rather less frequently back on to, all manner of weirdly adapted ships. From the triumphs and tragedies of those early attempts Captain Macintyre launches his enthralling story.

It is of course a pointless exercise to apportion to any single weapon, any more than to any single general or to any single country, excessive credit for its part in the war. Nevertheless there were certain aspects of the war upon which a great deal hinged, and the aircraft carrier war undoubtedly fell into that category; again and again the carrier emerged as the crucial element in the composition of the fighting forces, particularly where the United States was concerned. The attack on Pearl Harbor, which finally dragged the American nation into the war, was launched from carriers, and from that moment on they continued to appear in the starring role as the vital battles at sea were played out – the Battle of Midway, the Battle of the Philippine Sea, and the struggle for control of the Mediterranean. Even the battle between the U-Boats and the Allied merchant fleets which was fought from beneath the sea, was ultimately decided by carrier-borne aircraft flying above it.

Looked at from any standpoint, the unavoidable conclusion emerges that the aircraft carrier was a vital component in the vast array of battle machines with which both sides fought the war.

The aircraft carrier began by ousting from command of the seas the big ships carrying heavy guns. Now, it seems likely that the carrier is on the point of giving way, in its turn, to a new generation of weapons among the armoury of sophisticated missiles and rocketry which are now emerging. When it does finally bow out, the carrier will have enjoyed a glorious if brief reign – and it will at least, in that short time, have vindicated the gallant efforts of its early pioneers.

Captain Macintyre, who has enjoyed two careers, as a naval officer and as a distinguished writer of naval history, leaves nothing out of a fascinating story. That, primarily, is the appeal of this book.

Fairy Swordfish in landing trials

Genesis

The airplane, first successfully flown by the Wright brothers in 1903, was still little more than a powered kite, a fragile structure of wood, cotton fabric and wire when the idea of operating it from a warship was first given practical trial. Chief credit for it must be given to the American aviator Eugene Ely, though the far-sighted Captain Washington Irving Chambers, USN, who persuaded the US Navy Department to authorise the expense and risk of such an experiment, deserves to be honoured also.

An even earlier example of prevision of naval aviation was the prophecy of the French aviator, Clément Ader who has some claim to have antedated the Wrights' achievement with a flight of 50 metres in 1890 and another of 100 metres in 1891 with a steam-powered aircraft called the *Eole*. Both flights ended in crashes, however, which makes it seem doubtful that the *Eole's* flight could be called controlled. Further experiments with a twin-engined steam plane were less successful and Ader made no more. Nevertheless in a book entitled '*L'Aviation Militaire*' published in 1895, discussing the prospect of naval aviation, he wrote '. . . an aircraft carrier will become indispensable. Such ships will be very differently constructed from anything in existence today. To start with, the deck will have been cleared of any obstacles: it will be a flat area, as wide as possible, not conforming to the lines of the hull and will resemble a landing strip. The speed of this ship will have to be at least as great as that of cruisers or even greater . . . Servicing the aircraft will have to be done below this deck... Access to this lower deck will be by means of a lift long enough and wide enough to take an aircraft with its wings folded ... Along the sides will be the workshops of the mechanics responsible for refitting the planes and for keeping them always ready for flight'.

It was not, however, for another 15 years that aircraft were developed with which a trial of Ader's ideas could be made. During the year 1910, under the guidance of Captain Chambers, on the forecastle of the US light cruiser *Birmingham* there was super-imposed a platform 83 feet long and 22 feet wide, sloping down towards the bow at an angle of five degrees. Wilbur Wright was the first to be approached with an invitation to fly his aircraft off from this platform. When he refused, Chambers turned to another pioneer of aviation, Glenn Curtiss who agreed to allow one of his pilots, Eugene Ely, to make the attempt: His 50hp Curtiss biplane was therefore hoisted, early on 10th November, 1910, on board the *Birmingham* lying at anchor in Hampton Roads.

Overcast and hazy weather held up the trial until three o'clock that afternoon when there came a clearance. While the ship was weighing anchor, Ely hurriedly climbed into his cockpit and the ship had not yet gathered speed into wind at 10 knots, as had been arranged, when he launched himself at full throttle down the 57 feet of platform available for take-off.

His plane dipped as he ran off the end and actually touched the water just as he picked up flying speed. The splash splintered the tips of his propeller blades, but in spite of this Ely managed to get to a safe landing ashore. He had made history. Two months later he was to achieve an even greater claim to fame. He was to make the first deck landing.

Over the quarter deck of the armoured cruiser *Pennsylvania* had been erected a platform 102 feet long and 32 feet wide. Across this, supported by two fore and aft fiddles a foot high, 22 lines were stretched athwartships three feet apart, each with a 50-lb sandbag at either end. From the tricycle under-carriage of his machine, Ely had suspended three arrester hooks which, it was hoped, would pick up a number of these lines in succession and the cumulative drag would bring him to a halt. If not, a canvas screen erected at the fore end of the platform would arrest him without too much damage.

The *Pennsylvania* was lying at her moorings in San Francisco Bay on 18th January 1911 when Ely made his attempt. In spite of the fact that she was lying stern to a 10-knot wind, increasing his touch-down speed from 30 to 40 mph, he caught the twelfth transverse line with his hooks and was brought safely to a halt after a run of 80 feet. Forty-five minutes later, to the cheers of the ship's company, he turned his machine round and took off again – on this occasion with no trouble at all.

This epoch-making event had a sad sequel. Ely, whose only reward for his exploit was a letter of appreciation from the US Navy Department, was killed in a flying accident soon afterwards. The idea of operating aeroplanes from the decks of American warships was not followed up until another nine years had passed. Efforts were to be concentrated instead on the development of planes which could alight on and take off from water and be stowed on board without too much interference with a ship's fighting capability.

The pioneer in this type of aircraft was Glenn Curtiss who first fitted floats to one of his aircraft and took off from the water on 17th February 1911, flew it to the *Pennsylvania*, landed alongside, was hoisted in and out again and flew back to his base at North Island, California. Detailed to study under Curtiss, Lieutenant Theodore G Ellyson, USN, learnt to fly and so became the US Navy's first qualified pilot.

The French, British and German Navies, developed an interest in aviation at much the same time. The last-named, profiting from the genius of Graf Zeppelin, concentrated on lighter-than-air craft and had no interest in aircraft carriers until a much later date.

The French Navy acquired its first airplane, a Farman, in September 1910 and detailed seven officers to learn to fly. A French aviator, Henri Fabre, took a float-plane off and alighted again on the Etang de Berre, near Marseilles, in the latter part of 1910. It was not until 1914, however, that a French warship was adapted to operate aircraft. This was the old cruiser *Foudre* on which was erected a hangar and a flying-off platform from which the aviator René Caudron made the first take-off in the harbour of St. Raphael on 8th May 1914. This was an isolated event, however, and the *Foudre* was normally to operate only seaplanes, hoisting them in and out by crane. French interest in aircraft carriers lapsed for the next eight years.

The British Admiralty's first interest in aviation arose from a jealousy of the advantage accruing to the German Fleet through its possession of Zeppelin airships for scouting. They therefore ordered a rigid airship of their own in 1909, officially designated the 'R.1', but unofficially the *Mayfly*, a name only too prophetically apt; for she was caught by a gust of wind and destroyed before she had ever flown, when being taken out of her hangar in September 1911.

Admiralty interest in lighter-than-air flight came to a halt for the time being; but in the meantime, inspired by the offer of the loan of two aeroplanes without charge by Mr Frank McClean and of free instruction by another member of the Aero Club, Mr G B Cockburn, they selected four officers to learn to fly at the Aero Club's field at Eastchurch in the Isle of Sheppey. They were Lieutenants Charles R Samson, Arthur Longmore and Reginald Gregory, Royal Navy, and Captain Eugene Gerrard, Royal Marine Light Infantry; they reported for their new duties at the beginning of March 1911.

Having learnt to fly the primitive box-kite aeroplanes built by the aircraft firm of Short Brothers, they turned to study how they might be adapted to naval purposes. They were too flimsy to take floats; instead air bags were fitted to the under-carriage and underneath the tail and on these one of them was successfully flown on to the River Medway in December 1911 by Lieutenant Longmore.

It could not take off from water, however; in the meantime, therefore, Charles Samson had been supervising the construction of a platform over the forecastle of the old battleship *Africa* and from this, on 10th January 1912, while the ship was in harbour, he flew off in the same biplane. Four months later Samson repeated the performance from HMS *Hibernia* as she was steaming at 15 knots.

Seaplanes of greater power and robustness were now coming from the Short factory. Experiments were made with mounting guns on them, 1½ pounders and even 6-pounders being tried; radio sets were fitted; and on 28th July 1914 Squadron Commander Arthur Longmore launched the first aerial torpedo, a weapon 14-inches in diameter and 800lbs in weight.

These aircraft had pontoon floats with which they could take off from the water, however, and consequently interest in launching aeroplanes from platforms waned in favour of adapting ships to operate seaplanes by hoisting them in and out.

The first of these was the old cruiser *Hermes* and though a trackway was built on her forecastle from which an 80 horse-power Caudron amphibian made several flights during 1913 while the ship was under way, she was later equipped with three Short seaplanes with folding wings housed in a canvas hangar forward. She was an early casualty of the First World War, being torpedoed by a U-boat in November 1914. The next was the *Ark Royal*, a tramp steamer purchased by the Admiralty in 1913 while in frame; and though she was re-designed to place machinery space, funnel and bridge aft, allowing a clear flying-off deck 130 feet long to be constructed, her low speed of only 10 knots was insufficient to create enough air speed over the deck for take-off by the more heavily loaded planes coming into service. She operated therefore as a simple seaplane tender, hoisting her planes in and out by crane.

With the outbreak of war, other ships were requisitioned for the same purpose. Speed to keep up with the fleet being an essential, fast packet boats on the cross-Channel or Isle of Man run were chosen, the first three being the *Empress, Engadine* and *Riviera*. From these a seaplane raid – the first offensive operation ever to be made by ship-borne aircraft – was mounted against Cuxhaven and Wilhelmshaven on Christmas Day 1914. The Isle of Man packet *Ben-my-Chree* was the next to be fitted out and she was sent to the Mediterranean where one of her Short seaplanes flown by Flight Commander C H K Edmonds made history by achieving the first success with an air-borne torpedo, a Turkish transport being sunk.

Although these exploits clearly demonstrated the naval implications of aviation, they did nothing to advance the introduction of what hindsight shows to have been the development of the future, the aircraft carrier on which aeroplanes could land and take off. The *Ben-my-Chree* had a forward trackway for launching seaplanes, but it was not used. Seaplanes carrying any useful offensive load required a bigger deck-space than could be erected on the little packet-boats; and though a much larger ship, the trans-atlantic liner *Campania* came to sea in 1916 with a complement of ten seaplanes which could take off, using detachable trolleys, from a forward deck, the seaplane, with its inability either to match the performance of land-planes or to land back on board was a dead end.

It was the former of these shortcomings of the float-plane, which made it incapable of playing a fighter role, that led to the first advances up the main stream of carrier development. From time to time the Grand Fleet, parading in the North Sea in all the pride of incomparable strength, was forced to submit to surveillance by the silver shapes of the Zeppelins floating invulnerable above.

This was more than the Royal Navy could stomach; and in 1915 the first steps to overcome it were taken. The Isle of Man packet *Vindex*, in addition to five seaplanes, carried in an after hangar, was fitted to carry two small fighters with wheel under-carriages which took off from a forward deck 64 feet long. The first ascent from this was made on 3rd November 1915 by a Bristol Scout biplane, It was not until August of the next year, however, that an opportunity came for action. Then Flight Lieutenant C T Freeman, RNAS, was launched to attack a Zeppelin by dropping Ranken incendiary darts on it. The airship got away but the practicability of such operations had been demonstrated.

Aircraft operated in this way, unless they were within flying range of a friendly airfield, had to be ditched on completion of their mission and retrieved, much the worse for the experience. That the · real requirement, if the Fleet was to have a satisfactory air arm, was appreciated, is shown by the fact that in this same month the Admiralty bought the unfinished hull of a liner, the *Conte Rosso*, which had been ordered by the Italians from the ship-building firm of Beardmore; but on which work had

been stopped at the outbreak of war. Designs were drawn up to give her a flush deck covering her whole length on which it was envisaged aeroplanes would both land and take off.

Appointed as a liaison officer between the Air Department of the Admiralty and the Director of Naval Construction was Commander Gerard R A Holmes an early enthusiast for the carrier concept. In August 1915 he had proposed the idea of a seaplane-carrying cruiser which had been rejected; but he was now able to influence the design of the first true carrier.

It was to take two years for this work to be completed, however; and in the meantime stop-gap measures of a less ambitious nature were put in hand. The packet-boat *Manxman* was taken up for conversion in the same style as the *Vindex*. Ironically, it was the serious shortcoming of a speed much below the reputed 21 knots of the *Manxman* that led the Admiralty to acquire a very lightly wing-loaded fighter to operate from her, the classic Sopwith 'Pup' which was perhaps the most popular aircraft to emerge on the Allied side during the war on account of its high manoeuvrability and ease of flying. Sopwith's were to go on to design the successful 1½-Strutter 2-seater plane for the Navy and the most respected fighter of the war, the Camel.

Two other passenger steamers which were taken over, the *Pegasus* (originally *Stockholm*) and the *Nairana*, each of which carried seaplanes aft and aeroplanes forward, were completed in August and September 1917, respectively.

Inducing the adoption of the 'Pup' had been the *Manxman*'s chief contribution to naval aviation. It was operating from other ships that this splendid little plane made its name. Powered by an 80 horse-power Le-Rhone rotary engine, with a wing loading of only 5 lbs per square foot and a power loading of 16.4 lbs per horsepower, it required a take-off run of only 20 ft into a 20 knot wind. Quite a small platform was required therefore and it was decided to erect one forward of the bridge of light cruisers, the first to be fitted being HMS *Yarmouth*.

The first flight from this platform was made in June 1917 by Flight Commander F J Rutland, the same officer who had made history when he piloted a Short seaplane on reconnaissance from HMS *Engadine*, accompanying Admiral Beatty's battlecruisers in the early stages of the Battle of Jutland, the first aircraft to take part in a fleet action. It was not long before the idea of operating fighters from cruisers paid its first dividend. On 21st August 1917 the *Yarmouth* was escorting a minelaying force in the Heligoland Bight when a the equipment not only of other light cruisers, in which a rotatable platform amidships came to replace the fixed platform forward, but also of battlecruisers. Here the platform was erected on the roof of one of the superimposed gun turrets. From that of HMS *Repulse* trained 42 degrees on the starboard bow, the first ascent was successfully made on 1st October 1917 into a 'felt' wind of 31½mph the pilot again being Rutland. By the beginning of 1918 all British battle cruisers had been so fitted. Soon afterwards the platforms were enlarged by portable

A Sopwith 'Pup' lands on *HMS Furious*. Note the manila rope arrester curtain

Zeppelin was sighted. The Pup was launched, flown by Flight Sub-Lieutenant B A Smart and clawed its way up to 7,000 feet unseen by the enemy. Gaining a position directly over the long, silver gasbag, Smart swooped and opened fire with incendiary bullets from his machine gun. Spectacular, flaming destruction of L22 was the result. An exultant Smart was picked up from his ditched plane by HMS *Prince* and was subsequently awarded the Distinguished Service Order.

This heartening success hastened planked extensions running along the big guns giving a take-off run long enough for the 2-seater reconnaissance 1½ Strutters. They made use of a quick-release device to allow them to develop full power before beginning their run.

These arrangements were, of course, far from ideal and raised problems of maintenance of the aircraft left exposed to salt spray and foul weather. It was obviously preferable to provide a special ship to carry the aircraft with a hangar for their stowage and a flight deck from which to take off.

Early in 1917 such a ship had been taken in hand for conversion. This was the *Furious*, one of the three curious brain-children of that imaginative innovator, Admiral 'Jackie' Fisher, 1st Sea Lord during the first years of the war.

She and the *Glorious* and *Courageous*, ships of some 19,000 tons, a speed of 31 knots and completely unarmoured, had been intended for operations inshore and in shallow waters for which purpose they each mounted a single heavy gun turret fore and aft – in the case of the *Furious* each housing a

having either to ditch their planes after each flight or, if possible, fly them to an aerodrome whence they could be laboriously transported back to the ship by road and lighter, felt challenged by the problem of landing on the deck. While the ship lay at anchor head to wind in Scapa Flow, they practised flying as slowly as possible up her side until, on passing the bridge, they could side-slip into the centre-line. With enough wind speed down the deck they should then be able to put a plane down on to it.

When the *Furious* put to sea on 2nd

A Sopwith 'Camel' takes off from the deck of *HMS Pegasus*

single 18in gun. The forward turret was now removed from the *Furious* and a hangar erected on her forecastle, the roof of which constituted a flying-off deck 228ft long and 50ft wide. A square hatchway in this deck permitted aircraft to be hoisted by derrick from the hangar where three seaplanes and five Sopwith Pups were housed.

With her high speed, the *Furious*, steaming into a fresh breeze, induced a wind-speed down her flight deck little less than the landing speed of the Pup. The pilots, galled by the inconvenience (to say the least) of

August 1917, the senior pilot, Squadron Commander E H Dunning, determined to try. He took the precaution of fitting a number of toggles to various suitable points of his plane and had his brother officers waiting to pounce and grab hold as he touched down. Dunning was successful at his first attempt, but not entirely satisfied with the performance because the catchers had grabbed the toggles while he was still just airborne. For the next attempt two days later he insisted they should wait until he had touched down. All would have been well, but as his wheels touched the deck, perhaps owing to a sideways drift, his starboard tyre burst. His plane slewed and before the catchers could get a good hold, it went over the side. Dunning was drowned. Further trials were forbidden.

The first deck-landing on a ship at sea had been made. The method, in truth, must be classed as something of a 'stunt' and hardly one for regular use by inexperienced pilots. It was right therefore, that some better arrangements should be devised. The correct solution, of course, was that advocated so long before by Clément Ader – a continuous deck free of obstructions. The problem of disposing of the funnel gases was being tackled in the design of the *Argus* but great difficulties were being experienced. As a short term solution, therefore, it was decided to withdraw the *Furious* again for a landing deck 285ft by 70ft to be constructed extending from her stern to her funnel. When she came to sea again in March 1918 with this addition, she also had additional accommodation for six aircraft

with extra workshops and lifts from the hangar to the flight decks. Her initial complement of aircraft was fourteen Sopwith 1½ Strutter 2-seaters and two Pups in accordance with current Admiralty policy that reconnaissance aircraft should be mainly provided by carriers, and that fighter aircraft should be operated from fighting ships.

Captain Wilmot S. Nicholson, the *Furious's* commanding officer, voiced the doubts of his pilots as to the practicability of landing on her after deck, pointing out that air turbulence from the funnel gases and bridge structure would make landing hazardous and that it would be a laborious business moving aircraft from aft forward along the narrow connecting gangways. He was to be proved right.

A form of arrester gear which had been successfully tried out ashore was fitted. It consisted of longitudinal wire cables held 9in above the deck and secured at each end. At the forward end of the deck was a wooden ramp under these wires. Projecting from the under-carriages of the air-

HMS Ark Royal

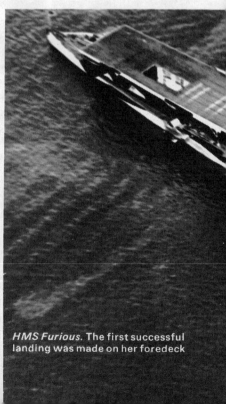

HMS Furious. The first successful landing was made on her foredeck

The first tragedy, August 4th 1917. Squadron Commander E H Dunnings's Sopwith 'Pup' goes over the side

craft, fitted with skids instead of wheels, were a pair of horns which were expected to engage in the wires. The primary purpose of this was to keep the aircraft straight after touchdown. To arrest it, laid across the wires athwartships were ropes attached to sandbags, as had been employed by Eugene Ely, to be caught up by a hook lowered by the pilot. Finally a curtain of manilla ropes was stretched across the deck to catch an aircraft if all else failed.

Fitted out in this fashion the *Furious* came to sea again in March 1918 and hoisted the flag of Rear Admiral P F Phillimore, the first Admiral Commanding Aircraft. Landing trials followed during which, out of twelve attempts only three were successful. The aircraft were bumped and buffeted as they made their approach and rarely touched down in a level attitude or on a straight course up the deck. Even the experienced Rutland went over the side into the sea and nearly lost his life. Furthermore the arrester gear usually failed to achieve its purpose and, as the head wind disappeared in the lee of the funnel and superstructure, even correctly landed planes often ended up in the rope barrier, suffering some degree of damage.

As a result of these experiences the use of the *Furious's* landing deck was abandoned. For the rest of the war she operated her flying-off deck only, from which on 19th July 1918 six Sopwith Camels took off to attack the airship base at Tondern, destroying the Zeppelins L54 and L60.

At about the same time as the decision was taken to give the *Furious* a landing deck, the first steps had been taken to provide other aircraft carriers. The 9,800 ton cruiser *Cavendish* of the *Raleigh* class which was nearing completion was modified by provision of flight decks forward and aft in the same manner as the *Furious* and she was re-named *Vindictive* when she came to sea in October 1918. The only landing attempted on her was quite successful; but by this time the requirement for a deck free of all obstructions had at last been fully accepted and, with the war at an end, she was placed in reserve and never again operated as a carrier.

Sopwith 'Pup' in the pen aboard *HMS Furious*. After the death of Sq-Cdr Dunning, only her flying-off deck was used

HMS Argus – the 'flat iron'. '. . . the first of a long line of seaborne airfields that were to change the face of naval warfare.'

A contract had already been placed in July 1917 with Messrs Armstrong for an ocean-going carrier *Hermes* of 10,850 tons, the first of such ships to be designed specifically as such. A few months later the battleship *Almirante Cochrane*, a 28,000 ton battleship which had been lying uncompleted for the Chilean Government since the beginning of the war, was bought and plans prepared to complete her as an aircraft carrier with an unobstructed flight deck 640ft long and 100ft wide. Re-named *Eagle*, she was launched in June 1918.

The chief interest at this time, however, lay with the *Argus* by this time nearing completion. Her debut was particularly looked forward to as it was known that Tom Sopwith had produced a successful torpedo-carrying aeroplane for carrier operation. This was the single-seater 'Cuckoo', powered by a 200 horse-power Hispano-Suiza engine, which could attain a height of 10,000ft, carrying a 1,000lbs torpedo in 25 minutes, at which height it had a speed of 87 knots. Orders for 100 of these aircraft had been given and delivery was to begin in June 1918.

Sir David Beatty, commanding the Grand Fleet had asked for 200 and had submitted a project to the Admiralty for an air offensive by the fleet against the harbour-penned High Seas Fleet. Although, in the event, the *Argus* only completed her trials less than a month before the Armistice brought the war to an end, the Board of Admiralty's rejection of Beatty's proposal must be recorded, the reasons given being a revelation of the lack of appreciation at that time by the naval hierarchy of the revolution in naval warfare that the aeroplane and the aircraft carrier had already initiated.

The response that came from the Admiralty after prolonged deliberation was that the results obtained by persistent heavy bombing operations made by the naval air units from their base at Dunkirk were not such as to encourage an air offensive against German bases by aircraft from carriers; all idea of an air offensive by Grand Fleet aircraft on German bases and ships in harbour must therefore be abandoned. This decision ignored the fact that the Dunkirk contingent

had no torpedo-carrying aircraft and that the lessons to be learnt from sporadic bombing of small targets were hardly applicable to a concentrated attack on the High Seas Fleet crowded in harbour. This under-estimation of the striking power of properly designed naval aircraft was tragically to persist and delay the full flowering of the British Fleet Air Arm in the inter-war years. Paradoxically, as will be seen, the effectiveness of other types of air attack on ships was to be so grossly exaggerated as to cast doubt on the viability of ship-borne airpower.

We are running ahead of our story, however. The lessons learnt from the *Furious's* deck-landing trials had been applied to the *Argus* where the original concept of an unobstructed flush deck had at first been impaired by the erection of superstructures on either side containing radio offices, crane machinery, cabins, etc., and joined by a navigating bridge carried on a girder construction some 20ft above the flight deck. Thus the deck had been virtually divided, as in the *Furious*, into two sections, one of which was intended as the landing area, the other for flying off. Now, however, these obstructions were removed, the fittings for navigating and working the ship being re-housed below the flight deck, while a small chart house was mounted on a hydraulic ram so that it could be lowered when flying operations were in progress and raised as necessary at other times.

As the vertical funnel had been replaced by two horizontal ducts running below the flight deck to discharge the gases over the stern, the flight deck was now entirely unobstructed and it was in this shape, which quickly earned her the sobriquet of the Flat Iron, that the *Argus* joined the fleet in the autumn of 1918, the first of a long line of sea-borne, mobile airfields that were to change the face of naval warfare.

Early development

The first deck-landings on the deck of the *Argus* were made early in October 1918 and before she became operational the First World War had ended on 11th November. Deck-landing was still in an experimental stage with the arrangements for arresting aircraft still of doubtful efficiency.

The method installed was similar to that which had been tried in the *Furious* though without the athwartship sand-bagged lines. The fore-and-aft wires were stretched between the upper edges of a pair of ramps so that the aircraft, which had their normal wheeled undercarriages, fell into a sort of shallow pit where hooks on the axle engaged the wires. When the plane reached the forward ramp and ran up it, the increased friction between the hooks and the wires acted as a brake and brought it to a halt.

This at least was the theory and, indeed, the early trials made with Sopwith Pups, 1½ Strutters and Camel were entirely successful. These very lightly loaded aircraft with their low stalling speed, however, needed only a short landing run even in still air; the *Argus* with her 20 knots available could reduce this to a few yards, making arrester gear hardly necessary and it was primarily to prevent a swerve over the ship's side that the for-and-aft wires were provided. When the *Argus* became operational her complement of aircraft was normally 15.

Meanwhile the *Hermes* and *Eagle* were being progressed. The latter in particular, posed some difficult problems in the matter of leading her funnel gases to discharge over the stern. In the hope of avoiding the necessity for such an arrangement, deck-landing trials were carried out on the *Argus* with a temporary superstructure erected on the starboard side of her flight deck representing a bridge and funnel. The pilots reported that this did not inconvenience them at all. It was decided, therefore, that both the *Hermes* and *Eagle* should be constructed in this way. The *Furious* on the other hand, which was now once again taken in hand for modification, was to have a similar arrangement to the *Argus*.

The *Eagle* and *Hermes* were completed in 1920 and 1923, respectively,

Landing practice on the flight deck of the aircraft carrier *Argus*. The early landing system, with hooks on the aircraft's axle, and wires which they engage, is clearly visible

the former carrying 18 aircraft and the latter 15. Both were equipped with similar arrester gear to that of the *Argus* except that the wires were supported by a series of hinged flaps which the wheels of the aircraft knocked down thereby inducing a degree of deceleration.

As heavier aircraft such as the Sopwith 'Cuckoo' single-seater torpedo plane and the two-seater Parnall 'Panther' spotter/reconnaissance aircraft were introduced, their greater weight and higher landing speeds made the defects of the system of fore-and-aft wires more apparent and of more consequence. The percentage of accidents varying from damage to undercarriages or tail skids to complete 'write-offs' steadily grew. A slight yaw on touch-down subjected the undercarriage to brutal stresses for which they had not been designed; often the wires caused a minor error to develop into a major accident. Nevertheless it was not until 1924 that it was decided to abolish the fore-and-aft arrester gear; and no alternative system had been devised.

For the next eight or nine years British naval aircraft landed on the decks of carriers relying only on the slowest possible touch-down and the wind down the deck to bring them to a halt. They had no brakes or steerable tail wheel to assist in keeping them straight during their landing run. Nevertheless the accident rate was less than with the fore-and-aft wires. To minimise the consequences of a swerve after touch-down, sloping palisades of steel stanchions with wire net stretched between them were erected on each side of the landing deck; aircraft which would otherwise have gone over the side were sometimes stopped by these with relatively minor damage.

Although deck-landing without benefit of arrester gear was satisfactory for the slow-landing types of aircraft of that period flown by pilots of above average skill, it was obvious that steadily increasing landing speeds must eventually call for some type of decelerating system. To put off that day, devices were fitted such as the variable camber gear in Fairey aircraft – the forerunner of flaps – and the Handley-Page slot on the leading

21

The *USS Langley,* converted from the collier *Jupiter* and commissioned in 1922

edge of the upper wing. This was held closed by the slip stream during normal flight but opened under the influence of springs as the stalling speed was approached and, by feeding air to the starved upper surface of the wing, reduced the stalling speed. But the absence of arrester gear undoubtedly delayed the provision of higher performance aircraft for the British Royal Navy.

The United States Navy had shown little interest in deck-flying until the end of the war. By that time only one ship, the battleship *Texas,* was equip-

ped even with a flying-off platform for wheeled aeroplanes from which a Sopwith Camel was occasionally operated. Not until 1919 did they decide to acquire a flush-deck carrier by converting the collier *Jupiter* and it was March 1922 before she emerged as the *Langley.*

Although the *Langley* was intended only as an experimental ship, with her top speed of only 15 knots she was not a good choice for conversion and made her utility of very limited duration. In 1937 she was relegated to the status of seaplane tender. This shortcoming

however, may have proved a blessing in disguise in that it forced an early development of an effective arrester system, whereas in the British Navy the 20 knots of the *Argus* and *Eagle* permitted a postponement. It took little time and a few trials with a fore-and-aft arrester system on the *Langley* to demonstrate the need for athwartships wires and for planes to be fitted with arrester hooks.

To solve the problem of disposal of funnel gases, the *Langley* was at first given a short funnel on each side, interconnected to discharge to port or starboard, depending on the direction of the wind. Later she was given two port-side funnels which hinged outwards into a horizontal position during flying operations. The first plane to take off from her deck was a VE-7-5F, a Vought biplane on 17th October 1922, piloted by Lieutenant Commander V C Griffin. Nine days later Lieutenant Commander G de C Chevalier who had played a leading part in experiments with arrester gear, made the first deck landing in an Aeromarine training aircraft.

These planes and others operated

during the next three years were conventional land-planes built by Aeromarine or Vought modified by strengthening their undercarriages and fitting arrester hooks.

From this time onwards US Naval Aviation under the able and enthusiastic guidance of Rear Admiral William A Moffett, the first head of the Bureau of Aeronautics set up in July 1921, forged ahead and the British Royal Navy which had established so commanding a lead in àviation began to fall behind in quality and quantity.

It seems extraordinary today that so obvious a necessity as some form of effective arrester gear took so long to be developed in the Royal Navy. This, however, was only one feature of the sloth which allowed it to drop behind not only the US but also the Imperial Japanese Navy. It can be attributed in some measure to war weariness and to the stringent economy enforced on a country financially ruined by the astronomical costs of more than four years of war, which restricted the operations of all types of unit, the new carriers as much as the rest. It was another circumstance however, which played the major part in bringing the development of aviation in the Royal Navy almost to a halt.

On 1st April 1918 the whole conduct of air operations, the provision of aircraft and of air personnel had been transferred from the Admiralty to the newly constituted Air Ministry. The aviators had been given the choice of remaining in the Navy or joining the new Service, the Royal Air Force. As the former would have meant giving up flying when the war ended, the majority chose the latter.

So long as the war lasted, the new arrangement made little difference except that the personnel found themselves changing their ranks and uniforms more than once, and during operations the captains of ships carrying aircraft no longer had the ultimate responsibility for the conduct or employment of the aircraft. But with the end of the war and the consequent drastic cuts in the armed forces, cuts so severe that the majority of defence projects had to be abandoned to keep a few with top priority alive, it was inevitable that the newly emergent Royal Air Force, fearful for its very continued existence, should resist expenditure on or divert its best personnel to what was to it a purely ancillary function.

The resultant neglect operated in a vicious circle. Almost no naval officers with any aviation experience remained; they assumed that the primitive aircraft provided for the fleet and the method of launching and recovery were the best available and that the lack of skill with which they were operated by landsmen pilots was simply a measure of the natural difficulties inherent in the novel art of flying. They tended therefore to discount the value of aviation to the fleet; this, allied to a natural conservatism of thought, led to an absence of any demand for improvement or of encouragement of activities which would bring such improvements about. Progress was thus very slow and intermittent and often misdirected.

So far as arrester gear was concerned, aircraft of greater ruggedness were required to stand the shock of deceleration suffered when hooking athwartships wires; but with responsibility for specification of aircraft entirely out of the Admiralty's hands, the necessary research and development was not undertaken.

Neither the US nor the Japanese Navy suffered in this way. Each retained control of its own air arm, though the former only did so by a narrow margin after fighting off a ferocious attack by the advocates of a unified air service led by General 'Billy' Mitchell, head of the Army Air Service. Mitchell made use of the sinking of various ancient warships and the surrendered German dreadnought, *Ostfriesland,* in bombing tests between 1921 and 1923 to launch a campaign in the press and elsewhere claiming that air power had made all warships obsolete.

No-one doubted that bombs could sink ships and so far as that was concerned, the conditions under which the tests were held were totally unrealistic. Hits were made certain and for the culminating test on the *Ostfriesland* the plan provided for observers to go aboard after each hit by a heavy bomb to assess the damage and the progressive disintegration. In the event, however, General Mitchell ignored all cease-fire signals after the first hit and his planes continued to pound the battleship with 1,000 pound and 2,000 pound bombs until she sank. Similar methods were used when Army bombers sank the old battleship *Alabama* in September 1921 and the 20-year old *Virginia* and *New Jersey* in September 1923.

All this time Mitchell kept up his feud with the Navy and his nation-wide publicity campaign for a unified air force. In November 1924 the Navy conducted its own scientifically controlled tests on the hull of the unfinished battleship *Washington*, scrapped under the terms of the Washington Naval Treaty. One thousand-pound TNT charges were detonated at varying distances, 400-pound torpedo charges exploded against her hull and fourteen armour-piercing shells dropped from 4,000ft. Not only did this fail to sink her but it took 2½ hours of shelling from turret guns before she finally went down, a proof that a ship constructed in accordance with modern ideas of armour protection and, in particular, internal compartmentation, was reasonably secure against bomb attack.

The results of this trial drove Mitchell to wilder attacks in which he accused the Navy of covering up the true facts. In the following year, however, he over-reached himself when, in commenting on the loss of the naval airship *Shenandoah*, he accused both the Army and Navy of 'incompetent, criminally negligent and almost treasonable administration'. He was court-martialled and subsequently resigned from the Army.

The agitation by airmen of the Mitchell clique was finally brought to nought by the findings of a Board set up by President Coolidge in September 1925 under the chairmanship of Dwight W Morrow which decided that the Army and Navy should retain control of their own air services, a decision whose importance in the light of subsequent history, it would be hard to exaggerate.

The wasteful effort which had had to be expended in combating the attacks of the Mitchell group had not prevented the US Navy from absorbing the true lessons to be learnt from the bombing tests, foremost amongst which was the vital part aviation had to play in the wielding of sea-power in both attack and defence. And to do so, it was clear, seaplanes and flying-boats, though they had their uses, had a strictly limited application. Only landplanes operating from that mobile airfield, the carrier, accompanying the fleet, could have the performance to provide air defence on the one hand and to strike the enemy effectively on the other.

Although, for the purposes of aerial scouting, seaplanes were to continue to be carried in battleships and cruisers of the American, British and Japanese navies – to be brought perhaps to their greatest utility and efficiency by the Japanese – it was the carrier that was to comprise the backbone of the aviation of these three foremost naval powers from this time onwards.

Even before the completion of the bombing trials, Admiral W S Sims, President of the US Naval War College, who had taken a leading part in the introduction of the dreadnought battleship twenty years before, had forecast that a fleet superior in aircraft carriers would 'sweep the enemy fleet clean of its aeroplanes and proceed to bomb the battleships and torpedo them with torpedo planes. It is all a question', he went on, 'whether the airplane carrier equipped with 80 planes is not the capital ship of the future'.

The Japanese Naval Air Service began with the training of six naval officers to fly in 1912; one of these was Chikuhei Nakajima, who was to become founder of the well-known aircraft manufacturing company of that name. The first aircraft with which the service was equipped were Farman floatplanes and they took part in the capture of the German colony of Tsingtau in September 1914, being operated from the seaplane tender *Wakamiya*.

During the rest of the war the Japanese Navy continued to operate only seaplanes, mostly Sopwith and Short types obtained from Britain, though Nakajima also produced at this time his first aircraft, a two-seater floatplane powered by a Salmson engine. The experience of the British in operating aircraft from

The *Lexington,* commissioned in 1927, was converted from a battle cruiser to take advantage of the terms of the Washington Treaty

flight decks inspired them to follow suit and in 1920 they applied to the British Government for the loan of an Aviation Mission. Serving officers of the Royal Air Force could not be spared but Colonel the Master of Sempill (later Lord Sempill), who had served in the RNAS, was recruited and he brought in a number of other ex-RNAS officers and warrant officers to form a semi-official Mission in 1921. Sempill's task was stated to be 'the re-organisation, equipment and training of the Imperial Japanese Naval Air Service'. This included advice on the types of aircraft required and the placing of orders for 200 machines with all the necessary equipment and spare parts for their operation.

At first the aircraft used were bought from English manufacturers, the ever-popular Sopwith 'Pup' being the first to be flown off from a ramp erected on the forecastle of the *Wakamiya* and from a gun turret of the battleship *Yamashiro* in 1920. Other types employed were the Gloster Sparrowhawk fighter, the Sopwith Cuckoo torpedo-plane and the Parnall Panther reconnaissance aircraft. But

the firm of Mitsubishi, with the aid of their foreign designers, such as the Englishman H. Smith, who came from Sopwith, was soon producing its own types, the first being the Type 10 fighter plane.

Sempill became a frank admirer of the Japanese as military aviators and when his Mission returned home he reported: 'The general ability in (Japanese) pilots is distinctly high, possibly higher than we are accustomed to find in this country, though it would seem likely that there is a smaller percentage of abnormally good pilots . . . The men are splendid, keen and hard-working . . . and will often forego leave without being asked in order to finish some work on hand'.

The Japanese had launched their first carrier, the *Hosho* on 13th November 1921. Completed in October 1922 she thus became the first carrier designed as such to come into service, antedating the British *Hermes* by nine months.

It was not until the end of February 1923, however, that the first take off and landing trials were made with a Mitsubishi Type 10 by the firm's test

The *Saragota,* also a conversion, was a sister ship of the *Lexington.* Both carriers in fact exceeded the Treaty limitations

pilot, Jordan, and the Japanese Lieutenant Shun-ichi Kara, while Lieutenant Commander Blackley of the Sempill Mission did the same with a Vickers Viking amphibian.

Though the *Hosho* was only 7,470 tons in displacement, her flight deck was nevertheless some 500 feet in length; she carried 28 aircraft and, with a speed of 25 knots, she was able to continue operating the naval aircraft of the day during the Second World War more than 20 years later.

As first completed in 1922 she had a small island on the starboard side housing the navigation bridge and signal mast, abaft which were three short funnels which could be swung horizontally over the side during flying operations. The bridge was removed in 1923, however, and the funnels were fixed permanently in their horizontal position, thus giving a clear flight deck from end to end.

An interesting feature was her system of mirrors and lights to assist pilots in landing. Though later Japanese carriers were not so equipped, it must be counted a forerunner of the system invented for the British Navy

in 1954 and subsequently adopted by carriers of the US and other navies.

When the Washington Conference on limitation of naval armaments was called in 1921, the position with regard to carriers was that Britain had two completed *(Argus* and *Eagle)* and two under construction or conversion *(Hermes* and *Furious)*; the USA and Japan had one each nearing completion *(Langley* and *Hosho)*. The terms of the Treaty which resulted included agreement to limit the total tonnage of carriers to 135,000 for Great Britain and the USA, 81,000 for Japan and 60,000 for Italy and France. The maximum size of individual carriers was to be restricted to 27,000 tons. The US Navy, however, wished to convert two of the battle-cruisers they had under construction, the *Lexington* and *Saratoga*, which would otherwise have to be scrapped. It was therefore agreed that any of the signatory powers might build two carriers of 33,000 tons. The Japanese also selected two uncompleted battle-cruisers for conversion, the *Akagi* and *Amagi*, but when the latter was destroyed in the great earthquake of 1923, the uncompleted

battleship *Kaga* was substituted.

Neither the French nor the Italians were enthusiastic about carriers; the latter built none at this time, while the French confined themselves to converting the uncompleted battleship *Béarn* into an island carrier of 22,146 tons. She could accommodate 40 planes but, like the similar British *Eagle*, her low speed of 21½ knots enabled her to operate only a fraction of this number.

The 33,000 ton limitation was actually impracticable for the effective conversion of any of the American and Japanese ships selected and all four emerged with considerably greater displacement. The Americans took advantage of a clause in the Treaty which allowed 3,000 tons more to each of them as battle-cruisers on account of improved anti-torpedo protection and the *Lexington* and *Saratoga* were of 36,000 tons displacement when they were commissioned in December and November 1927, respectively. That they had doubts of the legality of this increase is indicated by the official figure of 33,000 given out. The Japanese similarly announced the displacements of the *Akagi* and *Kaga* at figures far below the true ones which, when they were completed in 1925 and 1928 displaced 36,500 and 38,200 tons respectively.

As a result of this modification of the Treaty in respect of carriers, Britain, too, could have elected to convert two of the super *Hoods* which had been ordered. They decided instead to make use of the two near-sisters of the *Furious*, the *Courageous* and *Glorious*, the unarmoured, so-called light cruisers mounting four 15-inch guns which when converted would each displace some 22,500 tons. In the *Furious*, completed in 1925, and the *Courageous* and *Glorious* in 1928 and 1930 respectively, the flight decks did not extend the full length of the ship, stopping short to allow the upper hangar to become an open deck forward from which fighter aircraft, making use of quick-release gear, could take off.

By the end of the 1920's both the US

USS Ranger, a small carrier of 14,500 tons. She was never considered large enough to be effective

and Japanese Navies had caught up with the British in the number of carrier-borne aircraft they could operate, though in numbers of carriers they were still behind. To get a fair picture of the relative strength of the three air arms, it is necessary to examine the characteristics of the various ships and of the aircraft they carried.

A feature of British carriers throughout has been the inability, for one reason or another, to house or operate as many aircraft as contemporary American and Japanese ships. Leaving aside the *Argus* which inevitably suffered from the lack of previous experience, the *Eagle*, on a displacement of 22,500 tons carried only 18 aircraft. The *Hermes,* contemporary with the *Hosho* and 50% heavier, operated 15 aircraft as compared to the latter's 21. The *Furious, Courageous* and *Glorious*, each displacing about the same as the *Eagle*, were intended to operate 36, 52 and 52 aircraft, respectively, but found that 30 in the *Furious* and 36 in the other two was as many as could be comfortably handled.

In comparison, the *Lexington* and *Saratoga*, 36,000 tons, operated 72 aircraft each, the *Kaga* and *Akagi*, slightly larger, operated 60.

It would seem from these figures that British policy favoured a number of small carriers so as to give each of their fleets – Atlantic and Mediterranean – and their China Squadron a quota of ship-borne aircraft while the Americans and Japanese preferred to concentrate their naval air power in a few large units. This was not entirely so, however. Rear-Admiral Moffett, who disliked having half the carrier tonnage allowed by the Washington Treaty absorbed by two ships, suggested that the *Saratoga* and *Lexington* should be categorised as experimental ships and replaced by a number of smaller ones. The General Board disagreed and stressed the advantages gained by their great size and speed and pointed out that Moffett's idea would require an alteration to the terms of the Treaty. Nevertheless they asked Congress to authorise further small carriers of some 13,800 tons, one to be built each year. In the event only one was finally authorised, the 14,500 ton *Ranger* which proved to be the

29

The Yorktown, laid down in 1934 incorporated the 'island' design which became standard in United States carriers

least successful of any American carrier to be built. She was comparatively slow (30 knots) and was distinguishable from other American carriers by her small island structure and the three small funnels on either side which were interconnected.

While the *Ranger* was still on the stocks the decision was reached that 20,000 tons was the minimum effective tonnage for carriers.

The next two ships, therefore, the *Enterprise* and *Yorktown*, laid down in 1934, were of roughly this size, and with them the island design was finally made standard for US Carriers. With three lifts working between flight deck and hangars, they could each operate 80 aircraft. The turbo-electric drive which the Americans had up to this time favoured for their largest warships was discarded and replaced by geared turbines, giving them a speed of 34 knots.

Only 14,500 tons of the carrier tonnage permitted by the Washington Treaty now remained unused. A final smaller carrier of 14,700 tons, the *Wasp*, was therefore laid down. In these ships the hangars and flight decks, instead of being incorporated in the main hull structure as in the *Lexington* and *Saratoga*, were superimposed, fairly light structures. This was to make them and subsequent American carriers ill-protected against bomb

Three early Japanese carriers: 1. *Akagi* 2. *Kaga* and 3. *Soryu*

damage.

The Japanese carriers *Akagi* and *Kaga*, as they first emerged in 1925 and 1928, respectively, showed a distinct affinity with the British *Furious* in that the main flight deck extended forward only a little way beyond the small bridge superstructure on the starboard side, leaving a short flying off area at the fore end of each of the two hangar decks. Similarly the funnel gases were discharged through long exhausts extending right to the stern. Between 1935 and 1938, however, both ships were altered, each being given a main flight deck extending the full length of the ship and a rectangular funnel ·on the starboard side amidships at flight deck level, designed to discharge the smoke downwards and outwards. This funnel arrangement became the normal for subsequent Japanese carriers. The *Akagi* was at the same time given a bridge superstructure on the port side instead of the starboard side as in all other carriers. Each of these ships could operate some 60 aircraft.

The Japanese would seem to have at this time favoured the acquisition of numerous small carriers rather than a few large ones. The next carrier to be laid down, therefore, the *Ryujo*, completed in 1933, had a displacement of only 10,600 tons. Her flight deck and the two hangar decks below it did not extend the full length of the ship and left a low forecastle projecting forward of them. No superstructure obstructed the flight deck, the bridge being situated under its forward end. She could operate some 36 aircraft.

The permitted tonnage under the Washington Treaty had by now been actually nearly all absorbed, but the Japanese had consistently declared figures much below the true ones which ostensibly left them free to lay down the *Soryu* in 1934, which actually displaced 18,800 tons when completed in 1937 to operate 57 aircraft. The Washington Treaty expired in 1936 and the similar, but some 1,450 tons heavier, *Hiryu* was then begun, to be completed in 1939.

Such limitations as the apparent adherence to the Treaty had imposed were now discarded in the design of the next two Japanese carriers, the near-sisters *Shokaku* and *Zuikaku*.

With a displacement of 25,675 tons, and a speed of 34 knots, they could operate 72 aircraft. Both were completed in 1941 and were in commission in time for the outbreak of war with the United States and Great Britain in December of that year. One further carrier had been added in the meantime. This was the *Zuiho* of 11,262 tons which had been converted from an oil-tanker to operate 27 aircraft.

In comparison, the British did not even build up to their permitted carrier tonnage until they laid down the *Ark Royal* in 1935. Of 23,000 tons displacement and a speed of 32 knots she could operate 60 aircraft. Completed in November 1938 she was thus the only carrier in the British fleet that was not a veteran of the First World War, when the war with Germany began in September 1939.

This ship adopted the style inaugurated by the American *Lexington* and *Saratoga* of incorporating her double hangars and flight deck in the main hull structure, a practice which was to be followed in all subsequent British fleet carriers, such as the four 23,000 ton ships of the *Illustrious* class laid down in 1937 and the two similar ships *Implacable* and *Indefatigable* two years later.

The *Illustrious* and *Implacable* classes went further in that they were given stoutly armoured flight decks as well as armour-clad sides which virtually made armoured boxes of their hangars. Though this had disadvantages in respect of the number of aircraft they could accommodate and operate, it was to prove its worth in combat.

The Americans were slow to take advantage of the release from treaty limitations and it was not until September 1939 that they laid down the *Hornet*, similar to the *Yorktown*. Thus, although they went ahead rapidly after this, laying down eleven ships of the *Essex* class, the first of these did not commission until December 1942, and on the outbreak of war the US Navy had only seven carriers to the Japanese nine.

The *Wasp*, launched in 1939 was one of a distinguished line of United States vessels to bear the name

The approach to war

The number and size of carriers acquired by the three major navies gives one indication of their comparative progress in development of their air arm. More important, however, was the number and types of aircraft they could operate and the methods of employment they practised.

The British Navy, as we have seen, had a head start over the others in acquisition of carriers but progressed more slowly in provision of high performance aircraft. The two types of combat planes first provided, the Fairey 'Flycatcher' fighter and the Blackburn 'Dart' torpedo plane, had a performance adequate for their day; but the former, designed in 1922 remained standard equipment until 1935, when, in default of any aircraft designed for carrier operation, it was replaced by an adaptation of a land fighter, the biplane Hawker Nimrod.

The 2-seater Hawker Osprey – likewise an adaptation of a landplane – was also adopted, with the idea that, with its better navigational facilities, it should lead flights of Nimrods. The wide difference in performance of the two types made this unworkable, however, and both aircraft had only a short career in carriers, being replaced by the bi-plane Gloster Sea Gladiator or the dual-purpose monoplane Skua, mentioned later.

The 'Dart' was a single-seater torpedo plane and so lacked the navigational competence to strike at any useful distance from its carrier. It was replaced by the multi-seater Ripon in 1930, and later by the Baffin in 1934 followed by the Shark in 1935.

Nevertheless it was in the development of torpedo-plane tactics and of a reliable weapon for it, that the British Navy was least backward in the years between the wars. Massed attacks by planes from several carriers were practised and their effectiveness, in the absence of a strong fighter defence, spectacularly demonstrated.

But it was in the lack of a third type of plane, the scout-dive-bomber that the British Fleet Air Arm suffered most in comparison. Air Force belief in the high-level bomber, the effectiveness of which to attack ships at sea the Navy discounted, and failure to develop a dive-bomber, left it virtually with no bombing capability at all.

A torpedo being fitted to a Swordfish aircraft. In torpedo-plane tactics '... the British Navy was least backward.'

Instead, a multi-seater spotter-reconnaissance plane was provided. The task of spotting for the battleships' guns which was visualised for it, indicated lack of appreciation of the potential of the air arm in a Navy which still looked on the great guns as the prime battle-winning weapon. Even for these passive roles, the aircraft employed, such as the 'Blackburn', and the Avro 'Bison' had a lamentably low performance and endurance. They were replaced in 1928 by the Fairey III F and 'Seal' which for a time brought the standard up to a reasonable level for that day.

It was the failure to advance with the times and adopt monoplane types, however, which left the British Fleet Air Arm equipped with obsolete types at the outbreak of war in 1939. The only monoplane in service with the Navy at that time was the Blackburn 'Skua'. Originally intended to be a carrier-borne fighter, the Navy's demand for a dive-bomber and a desire to

reduce the number of types of aircraft carried, led to a combination of the two roles. As a dive-bomber the 'Skua' performed well. It is not surprising, however, that as a fighter it was inadequate and when war experience showed the overriding importance of fighter defence, it was soon replaced by a pure fighter, leaving the Navy once again without a dive-bomber.

The desire to limit the number of types carried, similarly led to the reconnaissance and strike roles being combined in a single plane in the 30's. The result was the 'Swordfish', widely known as the 'Stringbag', which was to accumulate a glowing record of achievements and a reputation for amazing versatility during the early part of the 2nd World War. These, however, were in spite, rather than because, of its performance.

A 3-seater biplane with open cockpits, fixed undercarriage and a top speed of 139 m.p.h., it achieved notable successes in operations against the Germans and Italians, neither of whom had naval air arms and so lacked fighter defence in the open sea. When the Swordfish or the Albacore – the closed cockpit version – were faced with Japanese carrier planes, their total inadequacy was at once exposed.

The British Fleet Air Arm's primary weakness, however, was its lack of control over provision of its own aircraft, training and equipment. This remained in the hands of the Air Force, which, born in a cloud of controversy and ever after fearful for its continued existence, clung jealously to its monopoly of all aviation matters other than the actual operation of ship-borne aircraft. Unlike the American and Japanese Navies, the naval aircraft on the outbreak of war was some 230 aircraft.

The Japanese, until recently, had the reputation of being borrowers or copiers of other people's designs. The aircraft adopted by their naval air arm in its early years certainly bore this out. Their first torpedo plane was the Sopwith Cuckoo as used by the British Navy, on which their naval pilots were instructed by the Sempill Mission. From it was developed the first Japanese-built carrier-borne attack plane, the Mitsubishi Type 13[1], designed by H. Smith and brought into

Fairey Swordfish – the 'string bag'. It accumulated a glowing record of achievements during the opening phase of World War II against the Germans and Italians, but was totally inadequate against the Japanese carrier planes. *Speed:* 139 mph.
Max range: 760 miles. *Armament:* two .303 inch Browning machine guns.
Bomb load: 1,500 pounds or one 18 inch torpedo

British Navy had to leave the training of its aviators and the development and provision of new aircraft to the sister service which was fully occupied in extracting the funds and producing the equipment for its own re-armament in the face of approaching war.

This was reflected in the number of planes under the Navy's control. By 1933 the Royal Navy still possessed only 159 aircraft in comparison with 1,000 in the US Navy of which nearly 700 were ship-borne, and 411 in the Japanese Navy.

The front-line strength of British

service in 1924. Powered by a Napier Lion 450 horsepower engine, it carried either one torpedo or two 530lb bombs. It remained in service until 1938 and was used in the Japanese attack on Shanghai in 1932. Another carrier-borne attack plane, the Mitsubishi

[1] In the first years of the Japanese aircraft industry, Type numbers indicated the year of the reign of the Emperor Taisho. Thus the Type 13 was first built in the 13th year of Emperor Taisho.

[2] From 1927 the Type Number is the last two figures of the Japanese date. Thus Type 89 was adopted in the year 2589 (1929 A.D.)

Type 89², built from a Blackburn design and powered by a Hispano-Suiza engine, was still in service in 1937 and, operating from the carrier *Kaga*, took part in the war with China – the so-called 'Sino-Japanese Incident'. The first attack plane of purely Japanese design and construction was the Aichi 92. All these were finally superseded by the Nakajima 97 in 1937, the world's first monoplane carrier-borne attack aircraft. Powered by a 770-1,000 HP Hikari air-cooled radial engine, it was capable of carrying either one torpedo or 1,760lbs of

and in 1936 the Mitsubishi Company developed their first monoplane fighter, the Type 96 (later known to the Allies as the 'Claude').

At the beginning of the 'Sino-Japanese Incident', Mitsubishi Type 89 attack bombers from the *Kaga* when raiding Hangchow suffered heavy casualties at the hands of defending Chinese fighters, composed at that time of British Gloster Gladiators, American Curtiss Hawks and Russian I-15 and I-16B. The *Kaga* was recalled to replace its Nakajima 90's with the new and as yet untried Claudes, which

Nakajima 97 – the 'Kate'. This was the world's first monoplane carrier-borne aircraft, and became the standard Japanese Navy attack plane of World War II. *Speed:* 235 mph. *Max range:* 1,238 miles. *Armament:* one 7.7 mm machine gun. *Bomb load:* one 1,760 lb torpedo

bombs, and was the standard carrier-borne attack plane during the 2nd World War, known to the Allies as the 'Kate'.

The first carrier-borne fighter to be adopted in 1921 by the Japanese was the Gloster Sparrowhawk; it was followed in 1929 by a Japanese-built version of the Gloster Gambet and known as the Nakajima Type 3. This remained in service until 1935, though a new Nakajima plane, Type 90 also came into service in 1930, followed by an improved version Type 95. This was the last biplane fighter to be adopted

thus gained the distinction of being the first carrier-borne monoplane fighters of any Navy.

They proved an immediate success and conferred air superiority on the Japanese. As the war advanced further inland, however, the limited range of the Claudes prevented them from accompanying the bombers. Casualties began to mount again. This added urgency to the need to produce an improved fighter and, in 1940, the answer came with the Mitsubishi Type 'O', the famous 'Zero' or 'Zeke' which so surprised the Allies by its

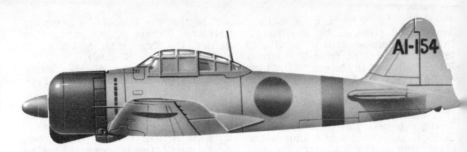

Mitsubishi Type O – the 'Zero'. Perhaps the most famous carrier-borne plane of the early years of World War II, it astonished the Allies by its endurance and reliability. *Speed:* 331 mph. *Max range:* 1,930 miles. *Armament:* two 7.7 mm machine guns, two 20 mm cannon. *Bomb load:* 264 lbs.

A Zero, captured at Buna, being tested for performance over the Australian countryside by an Allied pilot.

amazing performance and endurance at the beginning of the Pacific War.

The dive-bomber, the last of the three types to be adopted for Japanese carriers, was first introduced in 1934 with the Aichi Type 94 biplane based on a Heinkel design, which first saw service on board the *Ryujo*. An improved Type 96 was developed and remained the standard naval dive-bomber until the advent in 1939 of the monoplane Type 99, later known to the Allies as the 'Val', with which the Japanese carrier force entered the war. Capable of carrying 882lbs bomb load, it scored a number of spectacular successes.

Partly owing to strict Japanese security measures, but partly also to a Western disbelief in Japanese design capability, or, in spite of Sempill's flattering report, in the skill of Japanese aviators, this remarkable record in equipment of the Japanese naval air arm was not realised in Britain or America. It far outstripped that of the Royal Navy and was almost as far ahead of that of the US Navy.

Active service during the Sino-Japanese Incident, in which naval dive-bombers took part in support of the Army, as well as naval attack bombers in strategic – or more accurately 'terror' – bombing, gave the carrier pilots much combat experience and it was a highly-skilled, veteran force that delivered the opening blow of the Pacific War in December 1941.

US Naval Aviation began to equip itself with aircraft designed for carrier operation in 1923, the torpedo and bomber squadrons receiving the DT series of Davis-Douglas torpedo-bombers in that year. These were replaced over the next few years by the Martin torpedo-bombers powered by Pratt and Whitney air-cooled radial engines. All these were biplanes with performance similar to contemporary British torpedo planes. It was not until 1937 that the first American carrier-borne monoplane was accepted, the Douglas TBD or 'Devastator' with which the US Navy was to fight the first two years of the war with Japan. Its performance was considerably less than the Japanese contemporary 'Kate' and it was to be further handicapped by a slow and unreliable torpedo.

It was the Douglas company, also, that was to provide the navy's first monoplane dive-bomber, the 'Dauntless' SBD. This was to prove an excellent plane and it was to be responsible for nearly all the early successes of the American carriers, above all for the spectacular triumph when four Japanese carriers were sunk at the Battle of Midway. It came into service in 1940, superseding the series of Curtiss biplane Hell-divers with which the dive-bombing squadrons had been equipped since 1930.

The first monoplane fighter, the Grumman F4F or Wildcat also came into service in the nick of time, going into production in 1940. Grummans had begun to supply the US Navy with fighter planes in 1935 when they produced the biplane F2F with retractable under-carriage. Up to this time the fighter squadrons had been equipped with successive models of the Curtiss Hawk, powered, as was the Wildcat, by the Pratt and Whitney radial engine to which the US Navy was to stay faithful and which served it so well. Even the Wildcat, however, had a poor performance in comparison with the Japanese Zero which remained the best fighter in any Navy until the advent of the Grumman Hellcat in 1943.

The failure of the British Navy's Air Arm to advance into the monoplane age might have been disastrous but for the fortunate fact that both Germany and Italy had also adopted the unified air force and had virtually no naval air arm. Nevertheless, when the clash came with the opening of the Norwegian Campaign in April 1940, the lack of adequate fighter protection soon forced the British Fleet to operate outside the range of the Luftwaffe's dive-bombers, leaving the German fleet unopposed in the coastal waters of southern Norway.

Only in the far north, out of range of the Luftwaffe's Messerschmitt fighters was it possible for Swordfish from the *Furious* to make some ineffective bombing sorties early in the campaign while the Skuas and biplane Sea Gladiators of the *Ark Royal* and *Glorious* provided some fighter protection for the ships and troops engaged in the ill-fated expeditions to

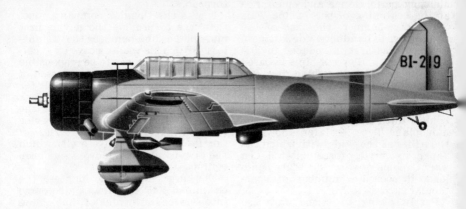

Aichi D3A2 dive-bomber – the 'Val'. Piloted by highly skilled veterans who
had gained vast experience in China, these planes dealt the opening blows at Pearl
Harbour. *Speed:* 266 mph. *Max range:* 970 miles. *Armament:* two 7.7 mm machine
guns. *Bomb load:* 816 lbs.

Douglas TBD – the 'Devastator'. The first American carrier-borne monoplane, its
performance was considerably less than the Japanese 'Kate'. *Speed:* 206 mph.
Max range: 435 miles. *Armament:* one .30 mm machine gun, one .5 inch cannon.
Bomb load: 1,000 lbs or one 21 inch torpedo.

Namsos and Andalsnes in the Trond-heim area. The *Glorious* also trans-ported a squadron of RAF Gladiators which flew off to operate from a frozen lake only to be promptly destroyed when the lake was bombed. In the course of these operations the carrier planes shot down 20 enemy aircraft at the cost of 9 Skuas, though only one of the latter was actually lost in combat.

When these southern expeditions were withdrawn, the carriers were transferred to the Narvik area where they provided the only fighter defence until RAF Gladiators transported in the *Furious* and Hurricanes in the *Glorious* established themselves a-shore.

The Narvik's operations came to an end at the beginning of June 1940 and the *Ark Royal's* Skuas gave fighter cover to the withdrawal while the *Glorious* embarked the surviving Gladiators and Hurricanes. The latter had never before been landed on a carrier's deck nor had their pilots any previous experience of deck-landing. All eight of them landed safely, how-ever, 'an achievement' in the words of

the expedition's C-in-C, 'which de-served a better fate than which befell the gallant men who had carried it out successfully'. For, on passage back to Scapa Flow, the *Glorious* was intercepted by the German battle-cruisers *Gneisenau* and *Scharnhorst*, making their first sortie since being damaged in the first days of the campaign.

For some reason, perhaps lulled into a false sense of security by the im-munity enjoyed up to now, no scouting Swordfish had been sent up from the carrier and she was taken by surprise when the enemy, aided by the gun-nery radar with which they were equipped, opened accurate fire at a range of nearly 14 miles. The *Glorious's* escorting destroyers, *Ardent* and *Acasta*, screened her with smoke, but the German radar enabled them to continue to hit the unarmoured car-rier, sinking her within an hour of the action beginning. The destroyers then attacked with suicidal gallantry and, before they were both sunk, the *Acasta* succeeded in torpedoing the *Scharnhorst* forcing her to limp back to harbour and the German squadron to abandon their operations: but for this a catastrophe must have befallen the lightly escorted troop convoys running blindly into the ambush.

The loss of the *Glorious* was a shattering blow at the Royal Navy's air strength. The *Courageous* had been lost in the first month of the war, being torpedoed by one of the U-boats (U29) against which, with four destroyers, she was operating in what was later to be known as a Hunter/Killer Group. The Navy was now left with the *Ark Royal* backed by the veteran *Furious*, *Eagle*, *Hermes* and *Argus*, all more than 20 years old and the last three able to operate only a handful of aircraft, to provide its air component for ocean-wide operations against commerce-raiders as well as the two main theatres, Home Waters and the Mediterranean.

Inevitably, the available force had to be parcelled out in single units instead of being employed in carrier groups such as pre-war exercises had shown to be the ideal. The *Ark Royal* was allocated to the Gibraltar-based Force 'H' for operation in the western Mediterranean and the Gibraltar approaches where her first employment was in the lamentable operation against the ships of Britain's former ally in the harbour at Oran. The attacks by a few Swordfish with bombs and torpedoes confirmed the ineffectiveness of other than mass attacks, though the French battleship *Dunkerque* was damaged by the explosion of depth-charges in a ship lying alongside her which was hit by a torpedo.

In subsequent operations six Swordfish from the *Hermes* succeeded in obtaining a torpedo hit on the *Richelieu* berthed in the harbour at Dakar without loss to themselves, which put the battleship out of action for a year. But when, two months later, further attacks were made by Swordfish with bombs on the *Richelieu* and with torpedoes on two French cruisers, they achieved nothing, while Skuas similarly failed to score any hits with high-level bombing – an early demonstration of the ineffectiveness of this form of attack against ships. Nine British aircraft were shot down.

At the other end of the Mediter-

One of the few left . . .
HMS Ark Royal, her flight deck swept by heavy seas

ranean the British fleet under Sir Andrew Cunningham had for its air component at this time only the 17 Swordfish of the veteran carrier *Eagle* to take care of reconnaissance, anti-submarine patrol and strike duties and just three Sea Gladiators, flown by the senior Fleet Air Arm officer, Commander Keighley-Peach, and two Swordfish pilots to provide fighter cover, when they could be spared from their other duties.

The torpedo planes scored their first successes operating from a RAF airfield in Egypt when on the evening of 5th July 1940 they attacked the harbour of Tobruk, sinking the Italian destroyer *Zeffiro* and the 4,000-ton motor ship *Manzoni* and badly damaging another destroyer, the *Euro* and the 15,000-ton passenger liner *Liguria*.

Two days later Cunningham took his fleet to sea from its Alexandria base for a sweep of the central Mediterranean to cover the passage of two convoys from Malta to Alexandria. By pure chance this sortie coincided with one by the Italian Fleet in support of a convoy to Libya. Each C-in-C was aware, through submarine and air reconnaissance of the movements of the other. Cunningham steered to cut his enemy off from Taranto, while the Italian Admiral Campioni, enjoying a speed superiority, planned a running fight to draw the British ships through a submarine barrage and into range of intensive attack by shore-based bombers. The first fleet action in which carrier-borne aircraft took part was thus brought about on 9th July 1940, off Calabria.

As the British fleet during the 8th steered westwards past Crete, through what was soon to earn the title of 'Bomb Alley', it was subjected to successive bombing attacks by Italian shore-based planes flying at heights of over 10,000 feet. Although the bombs were accurately aimed and the attacks were repeated throughout the day, only one ship, the cruiser *Gloucester*, was hit and damaged. This first experience, wearing and demoralising to the crews of ships who discovered the ineffectiveness of their inadequate anti-aircraft armament, was nevertheless early demonstration of the equal ineffectiveness of high-level bombing against ships at sea and free to manoeuvre.

The *Eagle*, which seemed to be picked out for special attention, was repeatedly surrounded by bomb bursts but suffered only from near-misses. Her Swordfish which maintained anti-submarine patrols all that day and twice gave warning of enemy submarines, were sent out at dawn on the 9th to scout for the enemy who was soon located by them and by Sunderland flying-boats from Malta. By 11.45 the two fleets had closed to within 90 miles of each other and a striking force of nine Swordfish armed with torpedoes was launched. The *Eagle* was unable to supply scouting aircraft simultaneously to shadow the enemy, however, and as the Italian battle fleet made a large alteration of course just when the Sunderlands had lost touch, the striking force failed to find its main target. The first aerial torpedo attack in a fleet action was thus aimed at the rear ship of an Italian cruiser squadron. It is perhaps not surprising that neither the Italian gunners, who put up a fierce storm of fire, nor the equally inexperienced aviators achieved any results. The latter landed again on the *Eagle* at 14.34 and their planes were immediately re-armed and re-fuelled. At 15.45 they took off once again to attack.

Meanwhile the cruisers of the opposing forces had come in contact and engaged at extreme range but without result on either side. Three minutes after the torpedo strike took off, the British flagship *Warspite* sighted the Italian battle-squadron and engaged Campioni's flagship, *Giulio Cesare* at a range of 26,000 yards and was engaged in return by both the Italian battleships. At this distance, without the aid of radar, chances of a hit were small, but at 16.00 a 15in shell from the *Warspite* struck home at the base of the *Cesare's* funnel. Her speed was reduced to 18 knots and Campioni decided at once to break off the action, steering away towards the Italian coast under a vast smoke screen.

The scene as viewed by Lieutenant Commander Debenham leading the Swordfish formation was one of considerable confusion, not to say obscurity. When two large ships leading a column of cruisers emerged from the smoke, taking them for battleships, he led down to the attack. Not until he was fully committed did the fact that they were actually 8in cruisers became apparent and it was on the *Trento* and *Bolzano* that the attack was delivered, once again in the face of intense, but ineffective gunfire, confused by dense smoke, and once again without scoring any hits.

All the aircraft were by 17.05 safely back on board the *Eagle*, where another strike was being got ready. Before this could be despatched, however, the encounter between the two fleets had been brought to an end by, on the one hand, the Italian unwillingness to fight it out and, on the other, by the British inability to continue the chase of the retreating enemy further into his coastal waters covered by the full strength of his shore-based air force.

The Italian bombers first appeared on that day at 16.40 and for the next three hours kept up a series of heavy attacks in which the fleet flagship *Warspite* and the *Eagle* were the favourite targets, though the British cruisers and destroyers also had their share. No hits were scored though ships were often badly shaken by near misses. Fortunately for the Italians, those of their bombers which for two hours bombed their own fleet with equal enthusiasm, were no more successful.

Nevertheless, with the Italians plainly determined to avoid surface action and with no fighter defence for the British fleet, Cunningham would have been courting disaster to approach the Italian coast any closer; at 17.35 he gave up the chase and turned away towards Malta where the task of covering the convoys for Alexandria still awaited him, and where his destroyers entered harbour to refuel.

On the evening of the next day, the 10th, the *Eagle's* striking force of nine Swordfish was launched once again to attack Italian cruisers and destroyers reported in the harbour of Augusta, Sicily. Only one destroyer and an oil tanker were still there when they arrived at dusk, however. Both were torpedoed, the destroyer *Leone Pancaldo* being sunk, and the Swordfish all returned safely to the carrier.

The rest of the story of this operation is a tale of three more days of repeated bombing attacks on units of the fleet as 'Bomb Alley' was traversed. None

During 1940, the mere possession of carriers
enabled the British navy to dominate the Mediterranean

45

achieved anything, while the *Eagle's* Sea Gladiators, now that pilots for them could be spared, shot down five enemy aircraft for no loss to themselves. During 14th and 15th July the convoys and the fleet reached harbour at Alexandria safely.

This first fleet action in which an aircraft carrier took part, indecisive as it was and on a scale so very small compared to those which were to develop later in the Pacific, has been described at some length not only on account of its historic interest as the first of its kind, but because of the lessons which emerged with regard to a new form of naval warfare.

The absence of fighter cover by either fleet was, of course, a marked feature and the need for it was forcibly brought home to both. The Italian Admiral noted that such a lack in the presence of an enemy aircraft carrier – even what Admiral Cunningham described as an obsolescent carrier with only 17 Swordfish embarked – permitted the enemy to reconnoitre and shadow unopposed and to attack with torpedo aircraft.

There can be little doubt that the slow, defenceless Swordfish would have been massacred if Italian fighter aircraft had been present, while the achievements of the three outmoded Gladiator biplanes on the British side showed what might have been possible with more modern, multi-gun fighters.

The striking power of aircraft showed up badly in this action, the only damage inflicted on either side being the one bomb hit on the *Gloucester* out of many hundreds of bombs delivered, though the cumulative effect of numerous near misses on the ancient hull of the *Eagle* was to have serious consequences at a later date. The impression was gained that the effectiveness of the bomb had been exaggerated whereas, in fact it had not been fairly tested owing to the absence from either side of the dive-bomber.

As was to be painfully demonstrated later against this type of attack, seips, aircraft carriers in particular, were extremely vulnerable without adequate fighter protection and a greatly increased armoury of close range automatic guns. When the torpedo planes were operated *en*

masse and in conjunction with simultaneous dive-bombing, air attack became deadly. After this action the British C-in-C, after noting that high-level bombing was more 'alarming than dangerous', reported 'throughout the fleet a determination to overcome the air menace and not let it

Heavy dive-bombing attack on *HMS Illustrious* 100 miles off Malta

interfere with our freedom of manoeuvre, and hence our control of the Mediterranean'. Had he experienced the dive-bombing suffered by the Home Fleet off Norway or during the Dunkirk operations, and foreseen the intervention of the German Air Force in the Mediterranean campaign, he might have been less sanguine.

For a while, however, his hopes were encouraged by the addition to his fleet of the new carrier *Illustrious* at the end of August 1940, equipped with radar and the Fairey Fulmar 2-seater fighter. Although this adaptation of a land-plane under development for the

RAF was 50 knots slower than the Hurricane and 30 knots slower than the contemporary Italian CR42 bi-plane fighter, it was at least a big advance over the Gladiator and Skua and for the first time the Fleet Air Arm had an 8-gun fighter.

Italian high-level bombing was now

successfully countered and, operating from Alexandria, the *Illustrious* and *Eagle* were able to deliver a number of attacks on airfields in the Dodecanese using their Swordfish in the role of dive-bombers. These aircraft were highly vulnerable to fighters, of course, and the attacks were therefore delivered by night. When one of them, an attack on Maritza airfield on Rhodes, was delayed and overtaken by the dawn, four out of 13 *Eagle* Swordfish employed were shot down. The most successful of these operations was that delivered on Benghazi harbour on the night of 17th September 1940 by 15 Swordfish from the *Illustrious* in which two Italian destroyers were sunk and other ships damaged.

At the other end of the Mediterranean the *Ark Royal,* as part of Force 'H', supported a series of operations in which the *Argus* and *Furious* transported Hurricane reinforcements for Malta, flying them off from a position some 300 miles west of the island. In the course of these operations the *Ark Royal's* Swordfish made diversionary raids on Italian airfields in Sardinia.

Thus the possession of carriers, albeit equipped with aircraft of very limited performance, enabled the British fleet to operate in and dominate the Mediterranean during 1940, even though it was closely hedged round by enemy airfields.

Nevertheless such operations were carried out in the face of another constant threat, that of the superior Italian fleet based on Taranto the backbone of which were the two splendid new 15in battleships *Littorio* and *Vittorio Veneto,* and three fully modernised dreadnoughts. The Italians had demonstrated their intention of maintaining this fleet 'in being' as a permanent threat and not risking it in battle, during the action off Calabria and again on 30th September, when they refused action with Admiral Cunningham's much inferior fleet. The only way to counter this was by attacking them in harbour. The arrival of the *Illustrious* early in September had made this possible and plans to bring it about were now set afoot.

Birth of a new era

During the first year of the European war, naval aviation had proved disappointing in its capability to strike at the enemy's fleet. In home waters opportunities had been few, though naval Skuas of Nos. 800 and 803 Squadrons operating from a shore base in the Orkneys had brilliantly seized a fleeting opportunity to dive-bomb and sink the cruiser *Königsberg* in the harbour of Bergen, the first occasion of a major warship being sunk by air attack in war.

In the Mediterranean, the one encounter with the evasive Italian fleet had served only to emphasise the difficulty of striking effectively with a small number of slow torpedo planes, unco-ordinated with dive-bombing, even in the absence of defending fighters. The Swordfish was too slow and too defenceless to be a suitable plane for striking by day. Its flying characteristics, however, made it ideal for carrier operation by night, and night deck-landings with it and its predecessors had been a feature in British carriers since 1930. It was now planned to take advantage of this and of the arrival of the *Illustrious* (which

also brought the necessary long-range tanks for the Swordfish), to attack the Italian fleet in harbour at Taranto.

A further essential condition for success was reliable and up-to-date knowledge that the Italian fleet was in Taranto harbour on the selected date; this was now assured by the arrival at Malta of some Glenn Martin planes to provide photo reconnaissance.

In a rapidly expanding force such as the British Fleet Air Arm had been since 1938, opportunities for training pilots in night deck-landing had been few. The first requirement, therefore, was to give the necessary practice to Swordfish pilots of the *Illustrious* and *Eagle*. Enough to launch an attack with 30 aircraft were ready for the first chosen date – 21st October, 1940. A serious mishap then intervened. A few days before the chosen date a fire broke out in the hangar of the *Illustrious* which destroyed several aircraft. Others were damaged and saturated with water from the hangar fire-fighting sprays. Repairs caused the operation to be postponed until

Admiral of the Fleet Sir James Fownes Somerville, commander of the Royal Navy's Force H, based on Gibraltar

the next suitable phase of the moon in mid-November. The delay itself was not a misfortune, for it allowed photographic reconnaissance to build up a more complete picture of the situation at Taranto, from which was discovered the existence and location of barrage balloons and anti-torpedo nets.

In the meantime the cumulative effect on her venerable frame of repeated near-misses by Italian bombs caught up with the *Eagle*, inducing defects in her petrol system which made her unfit to play her part in the operation. Five of her Swordfish and eight crews were transferred to the *Illustrious*, therefore, before the fleet sailed from Alexandria on 6th November.

Operation 'Judgment', as the attack on Taranto was named, was to be the final phase of a complex operation involving the passage of reinforcements for the Mediterranean Fleet from the west through the Sicilian narrows and the covering of several military convoys between Malta, Alexandria and Greece. By 8th November the fleet was in the Ionian Sea where Italian air reconnaissance located it; but the bombing attack which followed had not to be passively endured as on previous occasions; three Fulmars from the carrier intercepted the bombers, shot down two of them and forced the remainder to jettison their bombs and flee.

Further attempts to bomb the fleet were similarly dealt with during the next two days, the Fulmars shooting down eight enemy aircraft and damaging others without loss to themselves. By the 11th the rendezvous with the reinforcements had been successfully accomplished and the various convoys sent safely on their way escorted by units of the fleet. At 18.00 the *Illustrious*, with her escort of four cruisers and four destroyers, was detached and steered to reach the flying-off position 170 miles from Taranto at 20.00.

Operation 'Judgment' had taken a further knock during the previous three days, however. Three of the

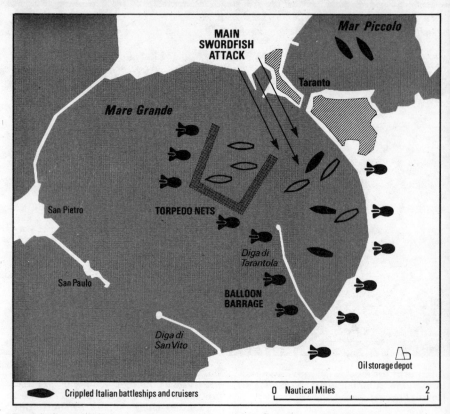

MAIN SWORDFISH ATTACK

Mar Piccolo

Taranto

Mare Grande

San Pietro

TORPEDO NETS

San Paulo

Diga di Tarantola

BALLOON BARRAGE

Diga di San Vito

Oil storage depot

Crippled Italian battleships and cruisers

0   Nautical Miles   2

Eagle's Swordfish flown off on scouting and patrolling missions had forced-landed in the sea. Examination of the remainder discovered contaminated petrol in their tanks. The number of planes available had been reduced to 21. Further modifications to the original plan had also been made as a result of the revelations of the reconnaissance photographs.

Taranto, the finest naval harbour in Italy comprises an outer and an inner harbour. The former (*Mar Grande*) is a semi-circular bay some four sea miles wide facing the west where the island of San Pietro and the smaller San Paulo, joined by breakwaters, close it except for the single entrance between San Paulo and the breakwater (the *Diga di San Vito*), reaching out from the southern shore. Another breakwater (the *Diga di Tarantola*) further eastward, also runs out from the southern shore for 1½ miles, partially enclosing the main fleet anchorage.

From the north-eastern shore of the *Mar Grande*, a narrow canal, passing through the town of Taranto, leads to the inner, land-locked harbour, the *Mar Piccolo*.

On the night of 11th November 1940, the whole Italian battleship strength, the brand-new *Littorio* and *Vittorio Veneto* and the four modernised older ships, *Giulio Cesare, Caio Duilio, Andrea Doria* and *Conte di Cavour*, were moored in the *Mar Grande* behind the *Diga di Tarantola* from the end of which stretched a double line of anti-torpedo nets. Close under the break-water lay three destroyers while between the two lines of nets were the cruisers *Gorizia, Zara* and *Fiume*. Four more destroyers lay to seaward of the nets.

In the *Mar Piccolo* the cruisers *Trieste* and *Bolzano* and four destroyers lay at buoys, the remainder of the destroyers and the cruisers *Trento* and *Pola* were berthed with their sterns to the wall of the dockyard on the south shore.

The Italians were fully alive to the possibility of such an attack as was planned and the recent daily visits of reconnaissance planes had further alerted them. Of the 12,800 metres of torpedo nets planned, however, only 4,200 metres had as yet been placed in position. A balloon barrage was in place close westward of the *Diga di Tarantola*, to the north-westward of the fleet anchorage and along the south-eastern shore of the bay. Sixty more balloons would have been in place if they had not been destroyed in a recent storm. Thus there were gaps in the barrage to the west, north and east of the anchorage.

The AA gun defences comprised twenty-one 4in batteries and some 200 machine guns of various sizes ashore and afloat, specially sited to oppose low-flying torpedo attack. Twenty-two searchlights were stationed on shore and on pontoons in addition to those on board the warships, all of which were kept in a state of readiness.

When the full extent of the net and balloon obstructions was revealed by the aerial photographs, restricting the dropping space available for the torpedo planes, it was decided to limit the number of these to six in each of the two waves of 12 and 9 in which the 21 aircraft were to attack. The remainder were to drop flares to the eastward of the *Mar Grande* against which the moored ships would be silhouetted or they were detailed to dive-bomb the ships in the *Mar Piccolo*.

Soon after 20.00 the *Illustrious* reached the flying-off position and, with the first wave of 12 Swordfish on deck, propellers whirling, turned into wind. The signal for take-off was given; the engine of the first plane roared and the Swordfish gathered way to become sluggishly airborne as it left the deck with its heavy load of torpedo and extra fuel. By 20.40 all were away and climbing ponderously up into a nearly clear sky with the light of a three-quarters full moon glinting on their silver wings. They were led by the squadron commander, Lieutenant Commander · Kenneth Williamson with Lieutenant N J Scarlett as his observer. At their majestic pace of some 75 knots they

rumbled off on the 2½ hour flight for their daunting target.

When still more than 30 miles away, the rippling flash of gunfire was seen as AA batteries on the south side of the harbour opened up with barrage fire in response to warnings of approaching planes by the sensitive listening devices. Now the course of the torpedo planes diverged from that of the remainder; the latter steered for the east side of the *Mar Grande* where the flares were to be laid, while the torpedo planes curved away so as to make their final approach from the west.

It was just 23.00 when the first flare blossomed in the sky, to be followed by a line of others. It was the signal for the torpedo planes to begin their long dive into the storm of gunfire which at once opened up from every part of the harbour. Three of them followed their squadron commander's line which led directly over San Pietro Island and thence through the southern line of balloons and over the *Diga di Tarantola* at a height of some 30 feet.

The balloon cables were miraculously avoided; the torpedoes were released, aimed at the nearest battleship, the *Cavour*. Two of the planes swung round to escape the way they had come, running the gauntlet of intense fire from the anchored ships, passing them a mere stone's throw away. They escaped unharmed; but Williamson's plane, the first to attack, had drawn the fire of too many guns; having released his torpedo which narrowly missed the destroyer *Fulmine* to run on and hit the *Cavour*, he splashed into the sea. He and Scarlett were taken prisoner.

Of the three other torpedo planes, one had taken a route which led between the two balloon barriers and had put a torpedo into the *Littorio's* port quarter; the other two had circled to pass round the northern balloon barrage to attack the same target, one of them scoring a hit on the battleship's starboard bow. All three planes survived the fire aimed at them from every angle, to escape to seaward and set off on the long flight back to the carrier.

Meanwhile the other six Swordfish of the first wave had been loosing their bombs on the ships and installations in the *Mar Piccolo*, attacks which were marred by the failure of many of their bombs to explode. Nevertheless they damaged the oil fuel depot, started a furious blaze in the seaplane station and acted as an effective diversion for the main attack.

The second wave of aircraft which had taken off an hour after the first were by now approaching, led by Lieutenant Commander J W Hale. They were only eight strong, five torpedo planes and three bombers, for one aircraft had had to return to the carrier when its external petrol tank had fallen off. They would have been only seven as one of the bombers had been damaged while being ranged on deck and had been struck down again for repairs. At the earnest plea of its crew, Lieutenants Clifford and Going, however, it had been allowed to take off alone, 24 minutes after the others and it arrived while the attack was in progress.

All the torpedo planes in this second attack came in from the northward. One attacked and hit the *Duilio*; two selected the *Littorio*, one of their torpedoes hitting her on the starboard side; a fourth, after recovering from flak damage that put it temporarily out of control, aimed its torpedo at the *Veneto* but missed. The amazing good luck which enabled all these to pass safely through the savage crisscross fire aimed at them, had run out when the fifth, flown by Lieutenant G W Bayley, with Lieutenant H J Slaughter, attacked. Blown to pieces it crashed near the cruiser *Gorizia*, both men being killed.

The bombers, after providing the illumination as called for by the plan, attacked the inner harbour only to suffer the same disappointing failure of many of their bombs, one of which hit the cruiser *Trento* and failed to explode.

By the time the last of these had completed its attack and turned to escape, the first of the earlier wave to return was circling the carrier, landing on her deck at about 01.20. During the next hour and a half, while all on board waited and anxiously wondered, one by one the Swordfish came droning back out of the night sky to be gathered in. That only two were

missing in the end and two of the remainder damaged seemed too good to be true.

At this small cost the Italian fleet had been crippled to an extent which, had it occurred in an old-fashioned sea fight between surface ships, would have been accounted a major victory for the Royal Navy. The proud *Littorio*, hit by three torpedoes, was awash forward and would be out of action for more than four months. The *Duilio* and the *Cavour* had both had to be beached. The former would be out of action until May 1941, the latter until

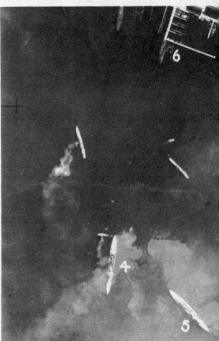

the end of the war.

Twenty-three years after Admiral Beatty's proposal to launch the Cuckoo torpedo planes of the *Argus* in an attack on the harbour-penned High Sea Fleet had been dismissed by the Admiralty, the new era in naval warfare had been launched. The events of that night over Taranto were noted with interest on the other side of the world in Japan, where the shrewd and far-sighted Admiral Isoroku Yamamoto was pondering how to minimise the risks inherent in the intentions of his government to make war on America and Britain.

Although the torpedo plane had thus justified itself as the most effective form of attack on capital ships, which were largely immune, by reason of their massive armour protection, from the largest bombs at that time in existence, it had yet to prove itself in action against ships free to manoeuvre. In June 1940 had come the first opportunity when the German battle cruiser *Scharnhorst* with a screen of destroyers, was located off the Norwegian coast.

The only naval aircraft immedi-

during the encounter with the Italian fleet in July, mentioned above, when the handful of aircraft from the *Eagle* had also been unsuccessful. That the chances of slow torpedo planes, attacking unsupported, of achieving hits were poor was to be yet again demonstrated in the same month as Taranto.

This time it was to be the aircraft of the *Ark Royal* of Force 'H' which were to be involved. This Gibraltar-based force under Admiral Sir James Somerville, engaged in covering a supply convoy on its passage through

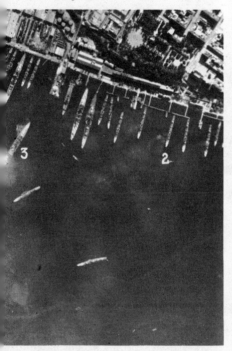 

ately available had been six Swordfish which had been operating from Hatston air station in the Orkneys engaged on anti-submarine patrol. They were too few for the massed attack that pre-war exercises had shown to be essential, and their crews were inexperienced. Nevertheless they were despatched and located the *Scharnhorst* after a 240-mile flight. But lack of surprise and poor tactics further reduced their chances of success; their torpedoes went wide and two of the planes were shot down.

The next opportunity had been

Above and above left: The inner harbour at Taranto, *Mar Grande* showing two Cavour Class battleships *at bottom, marked 4 and 5,* surrounded by patches of fuel oil

the central Mediterranean, was south-west of Sardinia on 27th November and about to make rendezvous with the old battleship *Ramillies* and two cruisers from the east when air reconnaissance from the *Ark Royal* reported the Italian fleet to the north.

Left: The batsman on *HMS Illustrious* brings an aircraft in to land. His violent arm action indicates a dangerous approach too close to the deck. *Above:* The Royal Navy at sea: a force of two aircraft carriers and a battleship, sailing together for mutual protection. The carriers' planes also vastly extended the battleship's range of vision.

Sending his convoy off to the southward, Somerville turned to challenge the superior enemy force – superior that is in everything except naval air strength. The opposing cruisers engaged at extreme range but neither side had achieved anything when the Italian Admiral Campioni learned of the presence of the *Ark Royal* and of two British capital ships; whereupon he at once turned away to refuse action, which with his superior speed he could easily do. This was in accordance with his directive from the Ministry of Marine. Since the debacle at Taranto, only two Italian battleships remained fit for action and no further reduction could be risked. Furthermore Campioni had much

respect for the capabilities of British naval aircraft, none for those of the *Reggia Aeronautica*. 'The British aircraft will damage our ships', he recorded gloomily, 'the Italian aircraft will not damage theirs'.

Somerville's only hope of bringing the Italians to action was to reduce their speed by air attack. A striking force of eleven Swordfish armed with torpedoes took off from the *Ark Royal*. They found the enemy battleships, *Vittorio Veneto* and *Giulio Cesare*, steaming in line ahead with a close screen of seven destroyers. It was a daunting target to attack out of a clear blue sky and made more difficult by a double reversal of course while the attack was developing. Admiral Campioni paid tribute to the resolution with which it was delivered, commenting on the difficult barrier imposed by the close line of destroyers, in spite of which the torpedoes were all dropped inside the screen. All were avoided by individual manoeuvres of the battleships though the airmen thought at the time that they had secured one hit. The return fire by the close-range weapons of the nine

enemy ships was intense but ineffective and the aircraft escaped unscathed.

Hope of forcing an action on the, fleeing enemy had clearly gone: with his convoy to think about, liable to massive air attack particularly at dusk, since the Italians had by this time developed torpedo planes, Somerville called off the chase and turned away to the southward. The *Ark Royal* was left free, however, to mount an attack on an enemy cruiser reported damaged and stopped. Captain Holland ordered a second torpedo strike to be prepared and on hearing of the imagined hit on one of the battleships decided to direct the torpedo planes against them while a flight of seven Skuas armed with bombs was sent after the cruiser.

This must be judged a tactical error. The experience of peace-time practices and the well-known principle of war calling for concentration of force both called for the whole of the carrier's striking power to be massed on the main target. Nine Swordfish only were available, made up from aircraft returned from reconnaissance and anti-submarine patrolling. Their crews were in need of rest after a long morning's flying; they were for the most part sketchily trained in the torpedo role. By the time they took off, the enemy battleships were close in to Cape Spartivento at the southern tip of Sardinia and passing under the protection of their shore-based fighters. The Swordfish had only some forty or fifty knots excess with which to overhaul the speeding enemy. The squadron commander had been given permission to vary his target at his discretion; so when the cruiser squadron of Vice Admiral Iachino was the first to be encountered he decided to attack.

Such highly manoeuvrable ships might perhaps have been hit if the aircraft had made a converging attack; but the best the inexperienced pilots could achieve was an attack in line astern all coming from the same side. A well-timed turn together by the cruisers caused all the torpedoes to miss. Once again all the planes escaped with only minor damage to two of them.

Meanwhile the seven Skuas had searched in vain for a crippled cruiser which, it seems, never existed. They located the other Italian cruiser squadron, however, and attacked, but failed to do better than shake the *Trento* with five very near misses. Had they co-ordinated with the Swordfish to attack simultaneously, it is unlikely that neither would have achieved anything.

It was now the enemy's turn to bring his air strength to bear. It came in the shape of the customary Italian high-level bombing in impeccable formation which attacks by intercepting Fulmars and Skuas failed to break up, though four Italian bombers were shot down and others jettisoned their bombs. The remainder flew on to concentrate their bombs on the *Ark Royal* with an accuracy that deserved better fortune that they actually enjoyed. The carrier more than once disappeared within a veritable forest of splashes, some of them less than ten yards from her, only to emerge unharmed.

With this the operation came to an end. The safety of the convoy assured, Force 'H' returned to Gibraltar.

After action, an aircraft carrier and its accompanying destroyer return to the Royal Navy's base at Gibraltar

The torpedo plane proves itself

By the end of 1940, British naval air squadrons had gained much and varied experience. Within the limited capabilities of their indifferent aircraft they had achieved a lot. In the strike role both Skuas and Swordfish had scored successes against warships, while the Gladiators, Skuas and Fulmars had played a not unimportant part in keeping the Fleet largely inviolate from bomb damage even when operating within easy distance of enemy shore air bases and out of reach of its own.

At the same time, however, the torpedo-plane had failed to achieve anything against warships at sea, while the handful of slow fighters which was all that could be operated from the single carrier normally available in any one force had been unable to break up the not very large formations of Italian bombers.

The small number in which the Swordfish had had to attack and the failure to co-ordinate their attacks with the dive-bombers accounted for their lack of success even against a fleet unprotected by fighters. Lack of numbers, even more than poor per-

formance had made the fleet's fighter defence ineffective. Only the Italian Air Force's preference for high-level bombing or, now that they were bringing torpedo planes into action, a failure to co-ordinate the two forms of attack had so far saved the Mediterranean Fleet and Force 'H' from serious loss, and permitted it to operate with impunity within easy range of enemy shore bases. This situation was now to change with dramatic suddenness.

The Germans had decided to go to the aid of their Italian ally in North Africa by sending the Afrika Korps under General Erwin Rommel. Before doing so, however, they determined that British naval domination of the central Mediterranean, across which ran the Axis lines of communication, must be ended and the fleet base at Malta eliminated.

Profiting from the Luftwaffe's notable lack of success in attacking ships during the Norwegian campaign, they had given special training to *Fliegerkorps X;* and in the last weeks of 1940 this powerful formation composed of 120 long-range bombers, 150 dive-

Swordfish lined up for take-off on
HMS Ark Royal. The carrier was to play
a vital part in the hunt for the
Bismark before herself being sunk by a
U-Boat late in 1941

bombers, 40 twin-engine fighters and
20 reconnaissance aircraft had been
transferred to airfields in Sicily.

At about the same time the British
Admiralty was preparing to send a
military convoy of five large supply
ships through the Mediterranean to
the Middle East. As on previous
occasions, the convoy was to be escorted as far as the Sicilian Narrows by
Force 'H' from Gibraltar and be met by
the Mediterranean Fleet beyond the
Narrows whence it would be escorted
to Alexandria. Such operations had
been entirely successful before and
there seemed no reason why this one
should be any different. Indeed, with a
modern carrier, *Ark Royal*, included in
Force 'H' and the *Illustrious*, fresh from
her triumph at Taranto, in Admiral
Cunningham's Mediterranean Fleet,
the British naval strength was at its
peak in the area. Furthermore the
Royal Air Force had by now been able

to deploy reconnaissance aircraft at
Malta with which to locate the Italian
fleet and give warning if they should
come to sea to dispute the passage of
the convoy. The limited RAF strength,
however, could not cover the whole
area nor could it supply any fighter
cover for the fleet. Swordfish from the
two carriers would still have reconnaissance tasks to fulfil while for
fighter cover the fleet would have to
rely, as before, on its exiguous force of
Fulmars.

Operation 'Excess', as it was called,
followed the familiar pattern of such
affairs as far as the approaches to the
Narrows, where Force 'H' and the
convoy arrived during 9th January
1941. During the afternoon the expected formation of 10 Savoia bombers
from Sardinia was duly detected by the
radar of the cruiser *Sheffield* and soon
they were circling to make their
bombing run from up sun, with the
guns of the fleet making a spectacular
display, while Fulmars from the *Ark
Royal* snapped round their tails. Two
of the Savoias would not face the gunfire and turned away, to be promptly
shot down by the Fulmars. The re-

59

mainder pressed on and dropped their bombs harmlessly into the sea, before escaping into cloud cover.

No further attacks came that day. The first part of the passage was safely over. At dusk all but three cruisers of Force 'H' turned back, leaving the convoy to thread the Narrows during the night. At dawn on the 10th it was met by the Mediterranean Fleet some 60 miles west of Malta.

Although a dawn attack by two Italian motor torpedo boats on the convoy had been foiled and one of them sunk, the day had begun badly for the Mediterranean Fleet when the destroyer *Gallant* had her bows blown off by a mine. While the *Mohawk* was taking her in tow, two Italian torpedo planes which attacked were forced by the ships' gunfire to drop their torpedoes ineffectively at long range. During the long tow back to Malta German high-level bombers came in two's and three's throughout the day, but in face of the gunfire of the three cruisers giving escort, they failed to achieve anything.

There was a different tale to tell where the main body of the fleet was giving escort to the convoy. Events there opened with a torpedo attack on the three heavy ships, *Warspite*, *Illustrious* and *Valiant* by two Savoia planes. Braving a storm of barrage fire by large and small guns, they delivered a determined and gallant attack but the torpedoes were avoided by a timely alteration of course. Four Fulmars which had been providing high cover swooped and chased after the Savoias to the westward.

It was at this moment, while they were away and using up their ammunition on the Savoias, that radar detected a swarm of aircraft gathering some 30 miles to the north. The fighters were recalled, the carrier turned into wind to fly off four more. She had just turned back on course when an attack such as had never previously been experienced by the Mediterranean Fleet began.

From the mass of some 36 Junkers 87 and 88 dive-bombers circling at 12,000 feet, flights of three peeled off to plunge seawards in converging attacks the majority on the *Illustrious*, brilliantly executed as their victims ruefully conceded. Though the ships

swerved this way and that in an effort to escape and though three of the dive-bombers were seen to be destroyed by the gunfire and the Fulmars shot down five more at the cost of one of their own, six 1,100lb armour-piercing bombs made direct hits on the *Illustrious*, wrecking her flight-deck, destroying 9 aircraft, setting her on fire fore and aft and inflicting heavy casualties.

The carrier was still steaming in circles out of control when a fresh attack developed, this time by the familiar Italian high-level bombers. Had they synchronised with the dive-bombers, they might have achieved something; as it was their bombs all fell wide. The *Illustrious* was got back under control and steered away for Malta. Two and a half hours later, dive-bombers again approached; but their losses in the first attack had no doubt unnerved them. Of the 15 Junkers in the formation, six would not face the fire of the few 4.5in guns remaining in action in the *Illustrious* and of the two destroyers of her escort. The nine which attacked did so with markedly less skill. Nevertheless one more bomb hit the carrier to cause yet more damage. The diminished *élan* of the dive-bombers was even more marked when 15 of them attacked the battleship an hour later. Received with a well-directed barrage-fire, they released their bombs at a greater height and scored no hits.

The *Illustrious* had taken savage punishment, but her armoured flight deck and the 'box' arrangement of her single hangar deck with its carefully designed petrol system undoubtedly saved her from the destruction which overtook less heavily hit American and Japanese carriers later. By the late evening she was in Malta and repairs were already starting.

The effectiveness of the dive-bomber if unopposed by fighters or the massed gunfire of a compact fleet was demonstrated again on the following day. The cruisers *Gloucester* and *Southampton* and the destroyer *Diamond*, none of which were equipped with radar, were steering to join a convoy from Malta to Alexandria when out of the sun plummeted a dozen Junkers, the first indication being the whistle of a bomb, the first of three to hit the

Scout planes take off from
HMS Ark Royal cruising under escort
in the Mediterranean

Force H escorting the old *HMS Argus,* with a load of
Hurricanes, through to Malta. A Swordfish is flying overhead

Southampton. She was damaged so severely and set so furiously on fire that after a long struggle to save her she had to be abandoned and sunk. The *Gloucester* was also hit by one bomb; but this, after plunging down through five decks, failed to explode.

The various convoys taking part in this complex operation passed safely through the central basin and on to their destinations. But the price paid by the Mediterranean Fleet made it clear that the arrival of the dive-bomber called for a much greater number of automatic guns in the ships and a more numerous and more effective fighter aircraft element than a single carrier could supply to put up a reasonable defence against them. It had ended British naval domination of the central Mediterranean for the time being. *Fliegerkorps X* turned their attention to Malta which was soon virtually neutralised as a base. Until high-performance fighters became available to the Navy and sufficient carriers were put in commission for several to operate in company, the fleet would only be able to function within range of enemy shore bases at an unacceptable risk.

While awaiting the arrival of the new carrier *Formidable* to replace the damaged *Illustrious*, which had gone to the United States for repairs, the Mediterranean Fleet, lacking any air support beyond the meagre effort the RAF could spare from the land operations, was confined to the eastern end of the Mediterranean. Meanwhile, at the other end, Admiral Somerville devised a novel way of trying to put his carrier's striking power to good use. As a diversionary feature of a plan to bombard the Italian ports of Genoa and Spezia, the *Ark Royal's* Swordfish were to launch torpedoes in Lake Tirso to breach the dam at its head which served the hydro-electric plant, Sardinia's main source of electric power.

The idea was a good one, as the destruction of the Moehne Dam in the Rhineland later in the war was to prove. Successful performance, however, required better conditions and better luck than the eight Swordfish met. Clouds hung low over the narrow, twisting valley of the Tirso River; rain and hail lashed the pilots in their

HMS Victorious, escorted by HMS King George V, flies off one of its Albacores

open cockpits and ice gathered on the wings. Furthermore the defences were on the alert and met them with an intense volume of fire. Only four torpedoes were dropped in the lake and none reached the dam. One of the planes was shot down. During the bombardment, postponed by the same foul weather, Swordfish bombed the refinery at Leghorn.

No opportunity presented itself, however, for a carrier-borne strike on enemy units at sea. This was to elude the *Ark Royal* for another four months. Before that the first success was to fall to the *Formidable*, which joined the Mediterranean Fleet on 9th March 1941. Like the *Illustrious* she had only a single hangar, enclosed in its armoured box, three to four inches of armoured deck above and 2½ inches below, 4½ inches of armour on the sides. The shortcoming of this design was the small number of aircraft she could operate – less than forty. Of these, the majority of her torpedo-reconnaissance planes were Albacores – biplanes with a performance not markedly superior to that of the Swordfish, but fitted with enclosed cockpits.

Since Greece had been drawn into the war by Mussolini's attack on her in October 1940, British supply convoys to the Piraeus and Crete had been regularly run under cover of the Mediterranean Fleet. By February 1941 the failure of the Italian invasion had led to a decision by the Germans to intervene on their behalf and they had begun to urge their Ally to use their fleet to intercept these convoys. The Italians resisted, protesting that, in view of the distances involved, the superior British air reconnaissance would enable them to counter any move. The only result would be a waste of oil fuel of which the Italian Navy was critically short.

Early in March, however, on receiving assurances of extensive co-operation by the German Air Force to provide air reconnaissance as well as fighter cover, and that two of Admiral Cunningham's battleships had been torpedoed (which was untrue), the Italian C-in-C, Admiral Iachino, was ordered to sea. His flagship, the *Vittorio Veneto*, six heavy cruisers, two light cruisers and attendant destroyers made rendezvous on the morning of 27th March to the eastward of Augusta and then proceeded in company towards Gavdo Island, south of Crete.

As Iachino had foretold, his force was promptly located by a Sunderland flying boat on reconnaissance; that evening, under cover of darkness, Cunningham led his fleet out from Alexandria to interpose it between the enemy and the convoy route to Greece. A dawn search by Albacores of the *Formidable* located the Italian cruiser squadrons and by 08.15 the Mediterranean Fleet cruisers, some 100 miles ahead of the main body were under fire from a division of 8in cruisers at extreme range. An indecisive running fight developed with the Italians falling back on their main body. This had not yet been located by the British reconnaissance, but the second division of Italian cruisers was reported steering for a position to cut off the outnumbered and outgunned British. A torpedo strike to ease the pressure on them was ordered. From the carrier's total of 10 Albacores, 4 Swordfish and 13 Fulmars, only six Albacores could be made available after the reconnaissance requirements had been met. By 1000, with an escort of two Fulmars, they were airborne with instructions to attack the Italian cruisers.

They were to find bigger game, however. For when they had been an hour on their way they sighted the massive bulk of the *Vittorio Veneto*, her 15in guns in action against the British cruisers who were now in a perilous position. The Albacores went at once into the attack and at 11.27 swooped down on the battleship in two waves, individual aircraft manoeuvring independently from converging angles through a daunting storm of gunfire, including heavy guns fired into the sea to raise a barrage of tall water spouts. The *Veneto* immediately began a circle to starboard which foiled the attack of the first wave coming in from her starboard side. This presented her port side to the last three Albacores, but the circling target was a difficult one and all torpedoes missed. Two Junkers 88's escorting the Italians were intercepted by the Fulmars which shot down one and drove off the other.

Once again the torpedo plane, employed in too small numbers, had failed to score. They had rescued the hard-pressed British cruisers, however, for the Italian Admiral, realising that he was opposed by a carrier and lacking the fighter protection his German allies had promised him, now only wished to escape. He steered away to the westward at high speed, dashing Admiral Cunningham's hopes of bringing him to action with his battleships, thrusting forward at their best speed but still far to the eastward.

A second striking force was ordered,

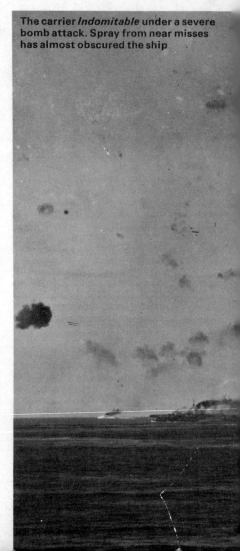

The carrier *Indomitable* under a severe bomb attack. Spray from near misses has almost obscured the ship

however. Again it was lamentably small – three Albacores and two Swordfish, escorted by two Fulmars. But they were to enjoy the support, fortuitously co-ordinated, of RAF shore-based bombers from Greece. Some of these aircraft – twin-engine Blenheims – had attacked the *Vittorio Veneto* while the torpedo strike was still on its way. They had achieved no hits, but they had introduced a new element in that apprehensive look-outs now anxiously scanned the upper air at the expense of the lower levels at which the torpedo planes approached. This, at any rate, was the explanation given by Admiral Iachino for the failure to sight the second torpedo strike until it was already diving and was down to 5,000 feet. Led by the squadron commander, Lieutenant Commander Dalyell-Stead, the three Albacores attacked from the battle-ship's port bow. As before, the helm was put hard over to turn the ship to starboard; but this time it was a fraction too late. Flying through the curtain of fire the three pilots dropped their torpedoes. The leader, to make certain of a hit, pressed in to very close range. He paid for his valour with his life, being shot down and killed at the very moment of release. The torpedo ran on to hit the battleship

near her outer port propeller, fracturing the shaft, blasting a hole through which 4,000 tons of sea water poured, and jamming her steering gear. The great ship slowed and then stopped to lie helplessly, down by the stern and listing to port. At about the same time, bombs from the Blenheims which had distracted the look-outs whistled down to burst near by.

The situation of the Italian flagship was now approaching the desperate, with three enemy battleships within three hours' steaming, though in fact Iachino, ill-served by his air reconnaissance was not sure of either the position or composition of the British squadron. The Italian engineers performed miracles, however. The steering gear was repaired and on her starboard shafts the battleship's speed was gradually worked up until she was doing 18 knots. It was enough to save her if no further damage was received. Against the probability of yet another attempt by torpedo planes, the admiral ordered his cruisers and destroyers to form a tight double screen round her.

This was the intimidating target that the *Formidable's* final effort – six Albacores and two Swordfish led by Lieutenant Commander W H G Gaunt and joined by two Swordfish from Maleme airfield on Crete – saw below them as they swept into the attack at dusk. Blinding searchlight beams, smoke screens and a dazzling crisscross of tracer shells and bullets combined to make utter confusion out of what followed. But when it was over and the aircraft had flown away to make for Crete on their nearly empty petrol tanks, the cruiser *Pola* lay immobilised, torpedoed on her starboard side.

The Battle of Cape Matapan, as it was to be called, might have ended there but for a fatal error of judgment on the part of Admiral Iachino. To determine the position of his pursuer he was forced to choose to rely either upon a report received from one of his reconnaissance aircraft or upon a 'fix' by shore radio direction finder stations which had been passed to him. The former had been so unsatisfactory up to now that he chose the latter which placed the enemy some 170 miles astern of him whereas the

actual distance was only 70.

On the strength of this he ordered the *Pola's* division mates, the *Zara* and *Fiume*, with four destroyers to turn back to stand by the crippled cruiser. Thus it was that in the black darkness of an overcast, moonless night the Italian squadron, not equipped with radar, steamed blindly across the bows of the British battleships to be blown out of the water in a few salvoes, only two destroyers escaping. The *Pola*, too, was sunk after her crew had been taken off, to complete a heartening victory for the Mediterranean Fleet.

It had been brought about by a mere handful of carrier-borne aircraft. The carrier-borne striking force had at last intervened effectively in a naval action in the open sea. The torpedo, the weapon favoured by the British Navy as the only one capable of sinking or crippling a capital ship, had justified itself and only the vicinity of the enemy to his own waters had prevented him from being brought, against his will, to even more decisive action.

That an attack by bombers, even though an ineffective one, had been synchronised with that of the torpedo planes, pointed the way to the correct tactics. Unfortunately the overriding need for a strong fighter force in the carrier and the comparatively small number of planes that carriers of the *Illustrious* class, with their single hangar deck and two lifts, could operate, had by now caused the retirement of the Skua from the scene, leaving the British Navy with the Swordfish and the Albacore as its only means of striking by air.

A strike plane with better performance and alternative roles as dive-bomber and torpedo plane, the Fairey Barracuda, was under development, but it was to be more than two years before it would come into operation. Looking into the future, too, it could not be forgotten that only the absence of fighter cover over the Italian fleet had enabled torpedo planes to press their attacks home.

Fortunately these conditions were also to hold good when next the Swordfish was to be asked to play a decisive role. On 23rd May 1941, the most modern and most powerful battleship in existence, the mighty

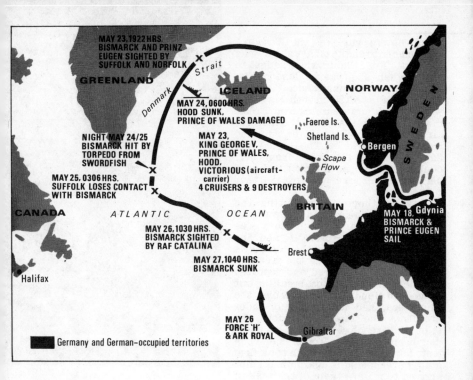

MAY 23, 1922 HRS.
BISMARCK AND PRINZ
EUGEN SIGHTED BY
SUFFOLK AND NORFOLK

GREENLAND

Denmark Strait

ICELAND

NORWAY

MAY 24, 0600 HRS.
HOOD SUNK,
PRINCE OF WALES DAMAGED

Faeroe Is.

Shetland Is.

Bergen

SWEDEN

NIGHT MAY 24/25
BISMARCK HIT BY
TORPEDO FROM
SWORDFISH

MAY 23,
KING GEORGE V,
PRINCE OF WALES,
HOOD,
VICTORIOUS (aircraft-
carrier)
4 CRUISERS & 9 DESTROYERS

Scapa
Flow

MAY 25, 0306 HRS.
SUFFOLK LOSES CONTACT
WITH BISMARCK

CANADA

ATLANTIC   OCEAN

BRITAIN

MAY 18. Gdynia
BISMARCK &
PRINZ EUGEN
SAIL

MAY 26, 1030 HRS.
BISMARCK SIGHTED
BY RAF CATALINA

Brest

MAY 27, 1040 HRS.
BISMARCK SUNK

Halifax

MAY 26
FORCE 'H'
& ARK ROYAL

Gibraltar

■ Germany and German-occupied territories

Bismarck, broke out into the Atlantic, putting Britain's vital transatlantic life-line in dire peril. The Royal Navy's entire available strength in home waters was mustered to destroy her – the battleships *Prince of Wales, King George V, Rodney* and *Ramillies,* the battle-cruisers *Hood, Repulse* and *Renown,* 14 cruisers and five flotillas of destroyers. They would have failed, with incalculable consequences to the war at sea, but for the intervention of two aircraft carriers.

The first contact with the *Bismarck* and her consort, the cruiser *Prinz Eugen,* was made by cruisers in the Denmark Strait who picked her up by radar and guided the *Hood* and *Prince of Wales* to an encounter which resulted in the loss of the *Hood* and damage to the *Prince of Wales.* In return the *Bismarck* received two hits neither of which endangered her seaworthiness or fighting power, but one of them, by piercing her oil tanks, forced her to abandon plans for operation in the Atlantic and head for the nearest French port with an adequate dry-dock, and reduced her speed to

28 knots. The other, apart from wrecking a dynamo, caused only a slight leak in a boiler room, but was to be of significance later.

With the main body of the Home Fleet, coming out from Scapa Flow, was the newly-commissioned carrier *Victorious* which had been on the point of leaving for Gibraltar with a large consignment of crated Hurricanes for the RAF. Her only operational aircraft were 9 Swordfish and 6 Fulmars. She was now directed to close to within 100 miles of the *Bismarck* and deliver a night torpedo attack. In low cloud and thick weather, with the aid of the newly developed air-borne radar, the Swordfish located her at a range of 120 miles and scored one torpedo hit on the zig-zagging ship.

The torpedo hit was amidships where the *Bismarck* was stoutly armoured and it did no damage in itself. But the high speed, drastic manoeuvres forced on the battleship in heavy weather aggravated the boiler-room leak caused by the shell hit. The boiler-room was flooded and her speed further reduced.

But now a ruse by the *Bismarck* enabled her to shake off her shadowing cruisers. For 31 hours she was lost to view. When she was at last re-discovered by a reconnaissance Catalina of the RAF at 10.30 on 26th May, she was only 11 hours steaming from Brest, much less than that from the massive air support which could be supplied from French airfields. The Home Fleet flagship, some 130 miles from her, could not intercept in time to prevent her escape unless her speed was further reduced.

Only one hope of preventing the *Bismarck's* escape remained, Pounding up from Gibraltar through heavy seas was Somerville's Force 'H' and the *Ark Royal*. Already the carrier's Swordfish were combing the area and at 11.15 they discovered and reported the enemy. The Catalina, breaking out of the rain clouds hanging low over the rough sea, had found herself under fire from the *Bismarck*. Before the pilot could reach cover again his plane had been damaged. Touch had been lost; but now the Swordfish took firm hold, never losing it again until ships arrived to relieve them of the task of shadowing.

For this purpose, Admiral Somerville detached the cruiser *Sheffield* of Force 'H', while on board the *Ark Royal* a torpedo strike of Swordfish was, not without difficulty, ranged on the carrier's wildly heaving deck. Unfortunately the *Sheffield's* mission was not conveyed to the carrier, so that, when the 14 Swordfish of the strike, flying through the low cloud and rain, detected a large unit on their radar and swooped to the attack, it was the cruiser which became their target. The *Sheffield's* prompt avoiding action prevented disaster; but they were chagrined pilots who landed back on deck to re-arm.

A second strike of 15 Swordfish, led by Lieutenant-Commander E Esmonde[1] took off at 19.10 and this time no mistake was made. Through the low clouds hanging over the target they dived. They were met by a tremendous volume of gunfire as they dropped their torpedoes at converging

[1] He was to die a hero's death and earn immortal fame and the Victoria Cross nine months later, leading a desperate attack on *Scharnhorst* and *Gneisenau* as they escaped up Channel for Brest.

Shells from a British warship score a direct hit on the *Bismark*

angles. Two hits, perhaps a third, were made; and one of them found the armoured ship's Achilles heel, her starboard quarter, damaging her propellers, wrecking the steering gear and jambing the rudders.

The *Bismarck* had become a helplessly circling cripple, her fate sealed at the eleventh hour. Through the night the wolves gathered round her and with the dawn they closed in for the kill. The *King George V* and *Rodney* pounded her to a ruin with 14in and 16in shells, leaving the cruiser *Dorsetshire* to deliver the *coup-de-grâce* with her torpedoes.

The waves closing over the perfect personification of the battleship era marked the supersession of the battleship by the aircraft carrier as the principal unit, the capital ship, of the fleet.

The destruction of the *Bismarck* marked the last German attempt to use their capital ships for commerce raiding in the Atlantic. Hopes of doing so were dispelled by the repeated damage inflicted on the *Gneisenau*, *Scharnhorst* and *Prinz Eugen* by RAF bombing raids on Brest where the

British Home Fleet and its carrier *Victorious* had no opportunities for fleet action, therefore.

In the Mediterranean Fleet, the *Formidable*, after providing air support with great success in the principal fleet operation of the early months of 1941, the passage of an important military convoy to Egypt, became one of the numerous sacrifices made by the fleet to support the Army in its defence of Crete against the German assault and to evacuate the ground forces when their defence was overcome. Her aircraft were thrown into the fight to attack enemy airfields. Operating close to these bases, the ship inevitably attracted the same sort of massed dive-bombing attack as had crippled the *Illustrious*. Though she was luckier than her sister ship in being hit only twice, the damage caused was too great for repairs to be made at Alexandria, and on 24th July the *Formidable* sailed via Suez for repairs in the USA. The Mediterranean Fleet was thereafter left to operate without a carrier, relying upon such air support as the RAF could spare, while paradoxically, disembarked car-rier squadrons from desert airfields assisted the RAF in attacking shipping in enemy held ports and in giving fighter cover to the Desert Army.

In the other half of the Mediterranean it was the presence of the *Ark Royal* that enabled Force 'H' to fight convoys through to Malta and to cover the passage of the older carriers, *Furious* and *Argus*, carrying fighter reinforcements for Malta. It was following one of these operations that the *Ark Royal*, returning with Force 'H' to Gibraltar, was torpedoed and sunk by *U.81* on 14th November, 1941.

The loss of this ship which had rendered such splendid and continuous service since the beginning of the war left Force 'H' emasculated. Although the *Eagle* and *Argus* joined it from time to time, they were principally employed carrying fighter reinforcements for Malta. No convoys could be run to the beleagured island. In March, 1942, Force 'H' itself was withdrawn to take part in the operation to capture Diego Suarez (Madagascar) from the Vichy French, in which the carriers *Indomitable*, *Illustrious* and *Formidable* all took part. In April and May the

HMS Victorious (left) and *HMS King George V,* two of the ships which took part in the hunt for the *Bismark. Far right:* Force H in the Mediterranean. *HMS Ark Royal (centre)* cruises with *HMS Renown* and *HMS Sheffield*

US's *Wasp* stepped into the breach to deliver Spitfires to Malta at the most critical moment of the island's ordeal, being followed by further reinforcement missions by the *Eagle* and *Argus* in May and June.

By June 1942 the plight of Malta was such that unless supply ships could be fought through, resistance would fail for want of fuel and food. Two convoys were organised, one from Alexandria escorted by the Mediterranean Fleet, the other from Gibraltar escorted by a Force 'W' in which the *Eagle* and *Argus* supplied the air support. The convoy from Egypt with no carrier to accom-

pany it, was forced to turn back as ammunition for the escorts' AA guns ran short and the Italian battle-fleet came to sea to intercept. That from Gibraltar, covered by a total of 16 Sea Hurricanes and 6 Fulmars from the two slow and antiquated carriers, from which never more than 8 planes could be kept in operation at any one time, fought off a succession of massed attacks by high level and dive-bombers and torpedo-planes escorted by fighters, to deliver two out of the six merchantmen of the convoy to Malta, relieving the fortress in the nick of time.

Far larger carrier operations had been taking place since December 1941 in the Far East; but none demonstrated more clearly the superiority of carrier-borne air-power over any other in defence of a fleet against air attack than this fight against tremendous odds. In theory no convoy should have been able to get through to Malta if simply the numbers on either side are taken into account. Only the presence of a self-contained, if pathetically meagre, ship-borne air defence force under the direct control of the fleet commander enabled a small but vital portion of this and another final convoy in August 1942 to do so.

But now we must leave the war in European waters, where a Navy equipped with a carrier-borne air arm had been opposed by two Navies dependent upon shore-based air power, to witness the clash of two Navies in the Pacific, each with a powerful carrier fleet and, for the most part, without the intervention of shore-based air power. It was to be a totally new concept of naval warfare.

' He was to die a hero's death and earn immortal fame and the Victoria Cross nine months later, leading a desperate attack on *Scharnhorst* and *Gneisenau* as they escaped up Channel for Brest.

Carrier meets carrier

The war which had erupted in the Pacific had its origins many years before when the Japanese had responded to the population explosion and industrial awakening in their country by expanding on the mainland of Asia. The occupation of Manchuria and the setting up of a puppet regime under the last of the Manchu Emperors had been the first step towards the setting up of the 'Great East Asia Co-Prosperity Sphere', in reality a vast Japanese Empire. It was followed, on a jumped-up pretext, by invasion of China – the so-called Sino-Japanese Incident – the naked aggression of which brought ever increasing sanctions against Japan by the United States and European powers.

Finally on 26th July 1941 these were stepped up to include a freezing of Japanese assets abroad, effectively drying up, for want of cash, all supplies of oil. A term was thus set – the period for which Japan could exist on her stored stocks of fuel and other raw materials – after which she must either relinquish all her conquests or go to war. There was never much doubt which the militaristic ruling clique would choose. Inspired by the patriotic-religious cult of Bushido, they could not realise that war with the United States, supported by her vastly larger industrial capacity, could only end in defeat in the long run.

One who did face this squarely, was Isoroku Yamamoto, C-in-C of the Japanese Fleet. Nevertheless he was confident that his highly trained fleet and particularly its air arm, perfected by three years of war with China, could win spectacular victories in the opening stages of war with an unprepared democracy such as the United States and with a Britain already fully-stretched by her fight with the Axis powers in the west.

To ensure this he knew he must first reduce the naval superiority of the American battle fleet: his chosen weapon was to be the naval air arm of which he had been the chief proponent and which he had seen grow in the last few years to six large and three smaller carriers with the most advanced fighting aircraft in the world. The British attack on the Italian Fleet

Admiral Isoroku Yamamoto, C in C of the Japanese Fleet.

at Taranto had made a deep impression. Early in 1941 a staff study was set afoot to examine the possibilities of a surprise air attack on the American Pacific Fleet in Pearl Harbor. By May a plan had been sketched out, guaranteeing success, provided that all the six large or 'fleet' carriers were committed to the enterprise and complete secrecy imposed.

The plan met with firm opposition from the Naval General Staff who insisted that the carriers were essential for the southward drive to seize the oil supplies of the Dutch East Indies which was to be the opening move of the war. Nevertheless Yamamoto pressed ahead with detailed planning and intensive, specialised training for the carrier squadrons. Torpedoes specially modified to avoid any initial deep dive on release into the shallow waters of Pearl Harbor were devised. 16in armour-piercing shells were converted into bombs for high-flying 'Kate' bombers.

It was not until 3rd November 1941, thirty-four days before the long-drawn diplomatic exchanges to find some other solution than war finally broke down, that the Naval General Staff at last gave its approval. A week later the first units of the fast carrier striking force under Vice Admiral Chuichi Nagumo slipped away from their anchorages for a secret rendezvous at Tankan Bay in the desolate, sparsely inhabited Kurile Islands. At the same time a force of sixteen submarines, five of which carried two-men midget submarines, sailed to co-ordinate their attack with that of the carrier planes.

Negotiations were still dragging on in Washington, though neither side expected any satisfactory outcome of them, when, on 26th November 1941, Nagumo led the six fleet carriers – *Akagi* (flagship), *Kaga*, *Shokaku*, *Zuikaku*, *Hiryu* and *Soryu* – to sea with their supporting force composed of two battleships, three cruisers, screening destroyers and eight replenishment tankers and supply ships.

Following a route well clear of all shipping, the planned flying-off position for the attack on Pearl Harbour would be reached at dawn on Sunday 7th December, coinciding with the

moment when the final breaking-off of negotiations in Washington would take place. The executive order for the attack would be signalled to Nagumo while on passage.

The fateful message reached him on 1st December. While his force completed its long ocean passage, negotiations were kept going and though their falsity was being exposed to the US Government through their ability to break the Japanese diplomatic cypher, no clear warning had reached the naval and military commanders at Pearl Harbor when, from a posi-

tion some 200 miles to the northward, the first wave of the Japanese striking force roared off the decks of Nagumo's carriers. It comprised 50 'Kate' bombers, each armed with a 1,760lb armour-piercing bomb, 40 more 'Kates' each carrying a torpedo, 51 'Val' dive-bombers carrying one 550lb bomb, and 43 Zero fighters to provide escort and deliver strafing ground attacks.

The first indication of enemy activity in the vicinity of Pearl Harbor was the detection of a sub-marine's periscope at 03.42 by a mine-sweeper on patrol off the entrance.

USS Shaw blows up as Japanese bombs find her magazine

At 06.45 that, or another submarine – one of the midgets – was depth-charged and sunk. It was not until some time after 07.25, however, that the alarm reached the naval C-in-C, Admiral Kimmel, and no thought of the possibility of an air attack had crossed his mind when, as he made his way to his office ashore through the stillness of a sunlit Sunday morning at 07.50, a bomb whistled down to explode on Ford Island, the naval air base in the middle of the harbour.

During the next thirty minutes Pearl Harbor, with its line of immac-ulate battleships, seven super-dreadnoughts lying with awnings spread in Battleship Row, and the fleet flagship in dry-dock, cruisers, destroyers and auxiliaries at their various berths scattered over the glinting blue waters, and Ford Island air base in the middle, was trans-formed into an explosion-rocked, smoke-shrouded scene of horror. Five of the battleships had been torpedoed as well as the cruisers *Raleigh* and *Helena* and the old target battleship *Utah* when the armour-piercing bombs from the high-flying

One of the few Japanese casualties
goes down in flames

'Kates' whistled down to plunge into the vitals of two of the battleships which had escaped the torpedoes by reason of their inside berths, and into two others.

Meanwhile dive-bombers had swooped on the Army and Marine Corps air bases where the aircraft drawn up wing-tip to wing-tip made perfect targets to be left in smoking ruin. They were followed by the Zeros which, finding no opponents aloft, were able to expend their cannon and machine-gun ammunition on ground targets.

By 08.25 the first wave had completed its attack and turned for home. There was a brief lull before the second wave arrived – 54 Kate bombers armed with 550lb bombs, 80 Vals and 36 escorting Zeros. Their main attack was concentrated on the dockyard where the fleet flagship *Pennsylvania* was hit and damaged and several destroyers wrecked.

When it was all over at about 10.00, 2,403 Americans had been killed, 1,176 more had been wounded; four battleships were resting on the bottom, another had been beached and the three others badly damaged. The battle squadron of the Pacific Fleet had ceased to exist. The cost to the Japanese had been 9 Zeros, 15 Vals and 5 Kate torpedo planes, out of a total of 354 planes engaged.

Nagumo was well pleased with the reports of his airmen when they landed back on board their carriers. Against the advice of his air group leaders, who urged a second attack, he turned his fleet away and steered for a replenishment rendezvous before returning to Japan.

There were two vital flaws, however, in the perfection of his success. The great naval yard and its oil storage tanks full of fuel had escaped serious damage; and amongst the ships attacked there had been no carriers. Of the three belonging to the Pacific Fleet, the *Saratoga* had been at San Diego, California, about to come west to join the fleet; the *Lexington* had been near Midway, delivering a Marine air squadron; while the *Enterprise*, returning from a similar mission to Wake Island, had been less than 200 miles west of Oahu. Some of the *Enterprise's* air group, indeed, had

USS Oklahoma has turned over;
USS Maryland burns behind her

arrived at Ford Island during the attack.

In the war which had been so spectacularly opened, the outcome was to depend not on the outmoded, slow, armoured monsters which had been the targets for Nagumo's torpedoes and bombs, but on the aircraft carriers able to strike, not at 20,000 or 30,000 yards with big guns, but at 300 miles or more with torpedoes and bombs. Thus the attack on Pearl Harbor, though it achieved Yamamoto's aim of preventing the American fleet from interfering with the Japanese southward drive to the East Indies and the Philippines, failed to gain any long term advantages. Indeed, by forcing the Americans to rely primarily on their carriers, it may even be said to have hastened the modernisation of the US Navy and the achievement of its supremacy in the Pacific.

The elimination of its battle squadron threw the US Pacific Fleet back on the defensive. The Japanese conquests of Malaya, the Philippines and the Dutch East Indies, which quickly followed, limited American aims for

the time being to the protection of the island chain from Hawaii to Midway and security of communications with Australia and New Zealand. For this purpose, carrier groups, each centred on one of the large carriers available, were formed. The *Saratoga* was torpedoed and damaged by a Japanese submarine on 11th January 1942 and returned to the States for repairs and modernisation. The *Yorktown*, however, had arrived from the Atlantic to maintain the number of groups at three with the *Lexington* and *Enterprise*. In the intervals between missions to cover convoys to the South Pacific they mounted air raids on Japanese bases in the Marshalls and Gilberts.

They were small-scale affairs, however, and ineffective compared to those delivered by the seasoned, powerful force under Nagumo which, operating as a fast, compact carrier force in support of the southward drive, hammered Rabaul in the Bismarcks and Amboina in the Dutch East Indies into surrender, and devastated Darwin. Then on 26th March Nagumo steered west into the

Indian Ocean to repeat the operation on Colombo and Trincomalee with five of his fleet carriers,[1], while the little *Ryujo* accompanied a force of cruisers on a commerce raiding foray into the Bay of Bengal.

Since the loss of Malaya and the destruction by a massed attack of more than 80 shore-based naval torpedo and bomber planes of the nucleus of a British Eastern Fleet, the battleship *Prince of Wales* and battle-cruiser *Repulse*, operating without fighter cover, the British had been assembling a fresh Eastern Fleet based on Ceylon. By this time a force had been gathered centred on the battleships *Warspite* (flagship of Admiral Sir James Somerville), and four of the *Revenge*-class, all veterans of World War I. They were completely outclassed by the Japanese battleships. Included in the force were the two modern carriers *Formidable* and *Indomitable* and the old *Hermes*; but the last of these was small, slow and carried very few aircraft; the two fleet carriers were not only able to operate far fewer aircraft than their equivalents in the Japanese squadron, but such aircraft

[1] *Akagi, Shokaku, Zuikaku, Horyu, Soryu,* with four fast battleships and two cruisers.

as they had were for the most part Albacores and Fulmars which would have been massacred if they had encountered Zero fighters.

Nevertheless this scratch force had been deployed south of Ceylon to challenge the Japanese reported to be approaching: it must be judged fortunate that, through a faulty estimation of the date of the expected attack, they had been obliged to return to their base in the Maldive Islands for replenishment when, on Easter Sunday, 5th April 1942, Nagumo's massed striking force swarmed over Colombo. Two of Somerville's cruisers, the *Cornwall* and *Dorsetshire*, steering to rejoin him, were discovered by Nagumo's scouting planes; within two hours they had been set upon by a swarm of Vals, smothered with bomb hits and sent to the bottom.

Somerville hurried his fleet to sea with the intention of minimising his aerial weakness by delivering night torpedo attacks on the enemy with his Albacores. Fortunately again, however, neither fleet located the other and Nagumo disappeared to return on the 9th to repeat his attack on the naval base at Trincomalee at the other side of Ceylon. The little

Hermes, with no aircraft embarked, was discovered at sea and overwhelmed by dive-bombers together with her destroyer escort, the Australian *Vampire.*

With these two demonstrations of strength, though in fact, except for the destruction of the two cruisers and the *Hermes*, they did little vital damage, Nagumo's carrier force had established a complete domination over the Indian Ocean. British capabilities of interfering with Japanese plans for the time being had been eliminated owing almost entirely to the hopelessly outmoded aircraft available for British carriers. The lesson had been painfully learned and steps to re-equip them with American types of naval aircraft were taken. The Grumman Wildcat was already coming into use and, before the Japanese were next encountered by the British Fleet Air Arm, would have been superseded by the Hellcat and the Vought Corsair. The Avenger torpedo plane was also on order, though in the event this was not to be employed in the torpedo role, the requirement for which had largely lapsed by the time the British re-entered the Pacific war.

Meanwhile, Somerville was forced

Far left: On December 10th 1941, the British ships *HMS Repulse* and *HMS Prince of Wales,* operating without fighter cover, were dive-bombed and sunk off Malaya. Here men of the Prince of Wales struggle to the safety of an escorting destroyer. *Above:* The end of *HMS Hermes,* 9th April 1942

ignominiously to retreat to a base in East Africa. The Japanese operation had however been intended only as a large-scale raid and Nagumo was now recalled to home waters where a grandiose plan to bring about a decisive battle with the US Pacific Fleet under conditions most favourable to the Japanese was being prepared.

In the Pacific the US Fleet had been thrown on the defensive not simply by the elimination of its battle squadron, which was too slow to co-ordinate operations with the carriers as the Japanese battleships could, but because of the American inferiority in carriers. Even the arrival of the *Hornet* in April left the C-in-C Pacific Fleet, Admiral Nimitz, with only four of these ships to cover the immensely long island chain of communications between Hawaii and Australia. This task was only made at all possible by the breaking of Japanese naval codes and the resultant advantage of knowing where the enemy planned to strike next.

Nevertheless there was to be staged one dramatic offensive act which would foreshadow the vengeance for Pearl Harbor to be ultimately exacted. In the *Hornet* her naval air group was stowed away in the hangars. On the flight deck sixteen US Army B.25's commanded by Lieutenant Colonel J H Doolittle were ranged. They were to be flown off some 650 miles from the Japanese coast and,

ambitious plan to expand the defensive perimeter of the homeland to the eastward and to bring the US Pacific Fleet to action. The outcome was to be the most decisive naval battle of the war.

Before this, however, and while the majority of Nagumo's carrier force was resting and re-equipping after its four months of ceaseless activity, an expedition to expand the perimeter southwards also was set afoot. The Solomon Islands were to be occupied and Port Moresby on the south coast of Papua captured whence Australia

Mitchell II. B.25. *Speed:* 284 mph at 15,000 feet. *Max range:* 1,525 miles. *Armament:* eight .5 inch machine guns forward firing and two .5 inch machine guns in the turret backward firing. For the Doolittle raid eight of the machine guns were removed to accommodate a 2,000 lb bomb load, and an extra 1,308 gallons of fuel

after unloading their bombs on Tokyo, were to fly on to friendly airfields in China.

On 18th April 1942 the bombers were launched from the deck of the *Hornet*, wildly plunging in a forty knot gale. Although the attack they delivered only inflicted a very moderate amount of damage, its shock effect on the Japanese people, who had considered their sacred soil inviolable, was tremendous; but its most important consequence was the impression made on Admiral Yamamoto, who now threw himself into support of a vastly

would be closely threatened. From the newly-established base at Rabaul, two occupation forces were to set out. A small force was to carry troops to seize Tulagi on Florida Island in the Sqlomons on 3rd May 1942 and set up a seaplane base, while a larger expedition to occupy Port Moresby would have a covering force of four heavy cruisers and the newly-completed light carrier *Shoho*, a ship of 11,262 tons converted from a high-speed oiler, which had 12 Zero fighters and 9 torpedo planes embarked.

The main covering force for the

whole complex operation was to be provided by the 5th Carrier Squadron, *Zuikaku* and *Shokaku* commanded by Rear Admiral Hara, and two heavy cruisers, the whole commanded by Vice Admiral Takagi. This seemed ample to the Japanese who believed that only one American carrier was stationed in the South Pacific. They were not to know that their plans had been revealed by cryptanalysis to Nimitz who, in good time, sent the *Lexington* group (Task Force 11 under Rear-Admiral Aubrey Fitch) to join the *Yorktown* group (Rear-Admiral

They found few targets remaining and the inexperienced pilots, many of them in action for the first time, achieved little. A destroyer and some barges were sunk and five seaplanes shot down for the loss of three of the carrier's planes. More important tasks awaited, however; in anticipation of the expected encounter with the enemy carriers, Fletcher returned south to join up with Fitch and with an allied force of American and Australian cruisers and destroyers under Rear Admiral Crace, RN.

During 5th and 6th May, Fletcher

The Doolittle Raid on Tokyo, 18th April 1942. A US Army B25 take off from *USS Hornet*

Frank Fletcher's Task Force 17) at the eastern entrance to the Coral Sea.

Rendezvous was duly made on 1st May and re-fuelling begun. Task Force 11 was still occupied with this when news of enemy moves began to come in. Leaving the *Lexington* group to complete, Fletcher headed north. On the evening of the 3rd, Japanese landings at Tulagi were reported and at dawn the following morning the *Yorktown* flew off a striking force of dive bombers and torpedo planes, followed by two further strikes during the forenoon and early afternoon.

waited for concrete information, on which he could act, to crystallise from the confused picture of scattered enemy forces which emerged from the reports of shore-based reconnaissance planes of General MacArthur's command searching the Solomon and Coral Seas. The area north of the carrier force was scouted by its own aircraft and these came near to discovering Takagi's squadron during the 6th, turning back just too soon. Takagi, in fact, had rounded the eastern side of the Solomons during the 5th and steered eastwards into the

Coral Sea, and then southward, groping for the single American carrier he expected to find. On the evening of the 6th he had turned north again to refuel which took him into the cover of a belt of low cloud stretching east and west across the Coral Sea.

Meanwhile some of the jig-saw puzzle of intelligence reaching Fletcher began to fall into place. Both the Port Moresby Invasion Group and its covering force were located and their future moves could be forecast. Sending Admiral Crace's force off to intercept the former if and when it came through the island chain off the eastern tip of Papua, and detaching his attendant tanker, the Neosho and her destroyer escort, the Sims, he shaped course through the night with his carriers so as to get within air striking range of the enemy at dawn.

At first light a flight of ten scout-bombers took off and fanned out over a wide arc between west and north. Those given the northern sectors were denied sight of Takagi's carriers by the bad weather shrouding them; but from the north-western sector came the long-awaited report of enemy ships, four heavy cruisers and two carriers at a distance of 225 miles. From the Lexington a striking force of 28 Dauntless dive-bombers, 12 Devastator torpedo planes with ten Wildcats as escort was sent on its way, followed half an hour later by 25 Dauntless, ten Devastators and eight Wildcats from the Yorktown.

Fletcher had thrown virtually his whole strike strength and most of his fighters into the attack. And who can blame him? For the first time two of the villains of Pearl Harbour were within reach of vengeance, it seemed. Unfortunately, however, his scouts had made a signalling mistake and, in fact, had only sighted cruisers and destroyers as Fletcher discovered when they landed back on board. Nevertheless that at least one enemy carrier was somewhere to the north west seemed certain; the striking force was not recalled.

While the American carrier force was in this vulnerable state, Japanese planes from Takagi's carriers were searching for it. Had they found it, catastrophe might have been its fate.

But a Japanese mistake counter-balanced Fletcher's. A scouting Kate sighted the Neosho and Sims and reported the former as a carrier. From the Zuikaku and Shokaku swarmed a strike of 36 Vals and 24 Kate bombers. They swooped on the two ships and sank them, expending their bombs at the very moment that Fletcher's real position became known to the Japanese admiral. Until his planes returned, Takagi could do nothing about it.

Fletcher had had better luck. His planes had sighted the little Shoho on which they concentrated their attack. Though some of her small force of Zeros tried to defend her, they were engaged by the Wildcats, which shot down eight of them; and the Shoho, dodge as she would, could not escape the co-ordinated bomb and torpedo attack. Thirteen bomb hits and seven torpedoes sent her quickly to the bottom. Only three American planes were missing when the exultant airmen returned to their carriers.

By the time all were gathered in, it was too late for Fletcher to mount an attack on the main force of enemy carriers even if he could locate them, and he decided to wait for the morrow. Takagi, whose experienced airmen had received training in night carrier operations, was less cautious. A strike of 12 dive-bombers and 15 torpedo planes led by Kakuichi Takahashi, who had led the dive bombers at Pearl Harbor, was sent off to make a dusk attack.

In the dirty weather they failed to make contact; with petrol running low they jettisoned their bombs and torpedoes and turned for home. Their route, unknown to them, took them directly over the American carriers. Radar detected them approaching and Wildcats were launched in the last of the light to intercept. The chagrined Japanese aviators, the target they had sought beneath them, found themselves under attack. Eight of the Kates had plunged into the sea before the remainder escaped as the Wildcats were recalled to land on before darkness overtook them.

Takahashi's men were to suffer further humiliation yet. Lacking radar or homing beacons they had difficulty finding their own carriers.

The *Shoho* — formerly submarine depot ship *Tsurugizaki*. Thirteen bombs and seven torpedoes sent her to the bottom. *Below:* The *Shokaku* under attack from United States Wildcats and Dauntlesses

Eleven ran out of petrol to splash into the sea; only seven, including Takahashi himself, landed back on board.

At the end of the first day of this first encounter between the opposing carrier forces, the score was clearly in the Americans' favour. So far it had only been skirmishing, however. The next day was to see the real clash.

Dawn saw the scouts of each side take off, the Americans from the area of clear blue sea, white-flecked by the trade wind, to the southward, the Japanese from where intermittent rain squalls were sweeping across. The opposing carrier squadrons were located almost simultaneously. From each a striking force was quickly on its way. 33 Vals, 18 Kate torpedo planes and 18 Zeros flew south, led by Takahashi in a compact body. The Americans total of 46 Dauntless, 21 torpedo planes and 15 Wildcats flew in two separate groups, that from the *Lexington* following ten minutes behind the *Yorktown's*.

When the latter arrived over the target, the *Zuikaku* was seen to disappear into cover of a rain storm; her sister ship bore the whole weight of the attack, therefore. It was well enough delivered, the torpedo planes co-ordinating their attack with that of the dive-bombers, while the Wildcats engaged the defensive patrol of Zeros. But this first sea battle of American naval aviation revealed a serious defect in their torpedoes; many ran wild, but all were so slow that, dropped well outside point-blank range by pilots experiencing massed gunfire for the first time, they were easily avoided. Two of the 500lb bombs dropped by the plummeting Dauntless found their target, however, heavily damaging the *Shokaku's* flight deck and setting petrol ablaze.

The *Lexington's* air group had meanwhile lost cohesion in the tumbling rain clouds and many, failing to find the enemy, had turned back. All but one of the Devastators managed to attack, but with the Wildcat escort reduced to six, five torpedo planes and three Wildcats were shot down, while the torpedoes proved no more effective than before. It was the Dauntless which saved the day. Though only four attacked, of which two were shot down, one more bomb-hit was

scored on the *Shokaku* causing further damage which sent her limping away out of action and raised the number of her killed to more than 100.

180 miles to the southward, the Japanese strike force found the American carriers, each the centre of a separate circular formation of cruisers and destroyers. Although the Americans enjoyed the advantage of

radar warning, fighter control had yet to be made effective and the swarm of Vals and Kates were unmolested as they swooped to the attack. A converging torpedo attack on the *Lexington* scored two hits while two bombs plunged through her flight deck, jammed her lifts and started fires. The *Yorktown* a handier ship than the huge 'Lady Lex', managed to avoid the eight torpedoes launched at her and escaped with only a single bomb hit which did no vital damage.

Both carrier forces had 'shot their bolts'. The first clash between the two air arms was over. Exaggerated claims by aviators on either side were inevitable; each side believed itself the victor. At this stage the immediate advantage lay with the

USS Lexington after the Battle of the Coral Sea. Petrol vapour from fractured fuel lines brought about her end

Americans. The damage to the *Shokaku* and the *Lexington* was about equal; both were out of action but apparently in no danger of sinking. The *Yorktown* had suffered some damage but could still operate her air-

craft, while the *Zuikaku* was untouched. But the Japanese had lost more than 40 aircraft during the day and many war-experienced airmen including Kakuichi Takahasi, while the Americans had lost 33. And the *Shoho* and more Japanese aircraft had been lost the previous day.

The situation was now to suffer a dramatic change, however. In the *Lexington* the several fires had been got under control, a seven degree list had been corrected by transfer of oil and, with her lifts jammed in the 'up' position, she had been able to gather in her returning aircraft and pack them on deck. But between decks an insidious peril had been creeping as petrol vapour from fractured pipes and tanks had spread. At 12.47 it reached a sparking electric generator; a violent explosion shook the ship.

It was the first of a number which started fresh fires while at the same time putting out of action the means of fighting them. By the late afternoon they were out of control; the ship might blow up at any moment. The order was given to abandon her and, at 18.53, torpedoes from a destroyer sent her to the bottom.

The loss of the *Lexington* turned the Battle of the Coral Sea into a tactical success for the Japanese. Though not apparent at the time, it was to prove a pyrrhic victory, however, the highly-trained Japanese carrier pilots lost being irreplaceable. Their loss as well as the damage to the *Shokaku*, were to keep the two finest and most up-to-date carriers out of service at the crucial moment of the Pacific War which was about to come.

Strategically, the Battle was the first Japanese set-back, marking, as it did, the checking of their ambitions to expand southward and threaten the Allied bases in Australia and the islands.

The Coral Sea also introduced the new face of naval warfare in which battles were won or lost without the opposing fleets ever coming within sight of one another. The ideas of Eugene Ely, of Clement Ader, Samson, Longmore, Irving Chambers, Moffett, Sims, and the early aviators who put their flimsy 'kites' down on the first carriers' decks had come to full maturity.

Incredible victory

Whatever the long-term consequences of the Coral Sea battle, the immediate situation for the C-in-C Pacific was one of extreme peril. With the *Yorktown* damaged and the *Saratoga* not yet operational after repairs and modernisation, he could dispose only of the *Hornet* and *Enterprise*. His cryptanalysts were able to tell him that the next Japanese move was to be an eastward thrust to occupy Midway Island, the northernmost of the Hawaiian chain, and the Aleutian Islands. All carriers were recalled to Pearl Harbor, therefore; but with only two of them, one manned by unfledged aviators, to oppose the five of Nagumo's experienced force known to be as yet undamaged, the odds were daunting. They were increased by Nimitz's lack of any fast battleships to accompany or support the carriers, whereas Yamamoto's fast battleship strength had just been raised to eleven by the addition of the mighty *Yamato*, the newest, biggest and most powerful in the world. Willy-nilly, Nimitz had only the largely untried weapon of naval air power in his hand. With it he prepared to counter the enemy's plans.

These called for the employment of the whole Imperial fleet in a vastly complex, typically Japanese operation by a number of separate forces. A Transport Unit of six troopships with a close escort of destroyers was to take 2,500 troops to occupy Midway Island. Providing support to this unit would be a force consisting of two battleships, four cruisers and a flotilla of destroyers and another advanced supporting force of four cruisers which were to bombard the island prior to the landing. These various units composed the Occupation Force.

A Striking Force, composed of the four of Nagumo's carriers available, *Akagi* (flagship), *Kaga*, *Hiryu* and *Soryu*[1] with an escort of two battleships, four cruisers, a light cruiser and destroyers, was to neutralise Midway's defences by air attack at dawn on the 4th June, prior to the landing.

The Main Body, under the personal command of the C-in-C in the *Yamato*, comprised seven battleships, two

[1] *Shokaku* damaged: replacements for *Zuikaku's* lost aircrews not yet trained.

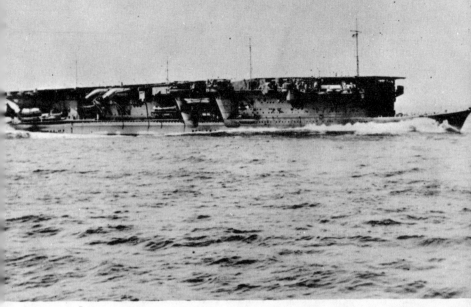

The Japanese carrier *Ryujo*, from which planes were flown to attack Dutch Harbour in the Aleutians

cruisers, a light cruiser and destroyers with the light carrier *Zuiho* and two replenishment groups. This force would be held back in a central position until the American fleet advanced to give battle.

Occupation of the Aleutian Islands of Kiska and Attu was an integral part of the plan to extend the Japanese defensive perimeter, but it was also to serve as a diversion from the main object and to lure American forces away from the principal scene of operations. A further diversion was to be provided on 3rd June by an air assault on Dutch Harbour in the Aleutians by a force including the small carrier *Ryujo* and the *Junyo*, a carrier of 27,500 tons newly converted from a passenger liner and capable of operating 48 aircraft. In the expectation that the Americans would react to the Aleutian threat by detaching part of their fleet, a group centred on four of the battleships of the Main Body was to be detached to the north-eastward to intercept. To give warning of any American northward sortie from Pearl Harbor, a patrol line of submarines was to be established to the north-east of Midway from 3rd to 7th June.

Much of this plan was known through cryptanalysis to the American C-in-C. That one of its main objects was to bring the inferior American Pacific Fleet to action was clear. To avoid this, while taking every opportunity to strike, was the basis of Nimitz's strategy; it was to be greatly assisted by the faulty Japanese deployment of their forces in scattered units.

On 26th May the *Enterprise* and *Hornet* (Task Force 16) arrived in Pearl Harbor. Its commander, Vice Admiral William F Halsey, an aviation specialist, laid low by a skin affliction, was relieved by the virtually unknown non-aviator, Raymond A Spruance, previously commanding the cruisers of TF16. On the 28th the Task Force sailed for a waiting position to the north-east of Midway.

In Pearl Harbor the *Yorktown*, which had arrived on the 27th with damage estimated to require several weeks of repairs, was a scene of unprecedented hustle as engineers and dockyard workmen swarmed over her.

By the 30th she had been patched up sufficiently to make her battle-worthy and she sailed as the flagship of Task Force 17 to embark her air group, made up by additions from the damaged *Saratoga* to 73 aircraft. Lessons of the Coral Sea were heeded and the proportion of fighters, as in the ships of Task Force 16, had been increased to 25 (27 in *Hornet* and *Enterprise*.)

By the afternoon of 2nd June the two forces had combined under the command of Rear Admiral Frank Fletcher in the *Yorktown*, thus evading the submarine patrol due to be set-up on the following day. No knowledge of their presence in the area reached the Japanese who, since 26th May, had been moving in their several separate groups towards their assigned positions, confident that the secret of their great enterprise had been preserved.

On Midway Island, a numerically strong air force had been concentrated. Seventeen Fortress bombers and four torpedo-carrying B26's of the US Army, 27 fighters (mostly obsolescent Brewster Buffalos), 18 Dauntless and 12 Vought-Sikorsky Vindicator scout-bombers of the Marine Corps and 6 of the new Grumman Avenger torpedo planes of the US Navy, jostled for space on the air strip. Many of the pilots were but partially trained; none had previously seen action.

In addition a squadron of Catalina amphibious patrol bombers, were based on the island and they and the Fortresses had been scouting daily to a distance of some 700 miles to the west and north. It was one of these Catalinas that raised the first alarm when, early on 3rd June, the Transport Unit was discovered 650 miles to the westward, though its composition was uncertain. When the Fortress bombers intercepted it that afternoon and attacked, the inexperienced army aviators identified battleships and cruisers as well as a large number of transports. Their bombs fell wide; nevertheless they believed they had hit several ships, leaving a battleship or cruiser and a transport ablaze and another cruiser damaged. During the night the attack was taken up by torpedo-carrying Catalinas, three of which attacked and scored a hit on a tanker which did little damage. Far away to the north the Japanese plan for 3rd June had gone off without a hitch. From the *Ryujo* and *Junyo* two waves of bombers had devastated Dutch Harbour. But if the news of it was intended to divert the attention of Admiral Nimitz from the main scene of operations and lure American battleships into battle with the four Japanese battleships detached for the purpose, it was a failure. Nimitz had sent a cruiser force to the Aleutians during May. With this, Rear Admiral Theobald in command of the area would have to make do until the main battle and been decided. Nimitz's force of slow battleships was retained on the Californian coast.

Yamamoto's Midway plan also opened to schedule. It called for Nagumo's Force to fly off its air strike at dawn on 4th June from a position 230 miles north-west of Midway, approaching that position from the north-west. As luck would have it, this route lay under a blanket of low cloud and poor visibility until after nightfall on the 3rd, shrouding the carriers from discovery. They were still unlocated when 36 Kate bombers from *Hiryu* and *Soryu* 36 Val dive bombers from *Akagi* and *Kaga* with 9 Zeros from each took off and, led by Lieutenant Joichi Tomonaga of the *Hiryu*, streamed away for the island.

They were more than an hour on their way before Catalinas, fanning out on their daily dawn search made contact and reported them. At 0552 the carriers themselves were located. Within a few minutes every serviceable aircraft on Midway was in the air, bombers and torpedo planes heading for the carriers, fighters clawing their way up to 17,000 feet. Thirty miles out from Midway the swarm of bombers in 'V' formation was sighted. The American fighters, 18 Buffalos and 7 Wildcats, swooped in attack; but in their turn they were caught by the Zeros, superior in numbers and greatly so in performance and experience. Every one of the Brewsters was shot down or severely damaged. Of the Wildcats three were destroyed and two damaged.

Few of the Japanese were shot down by them or by the island's AA guns; Midway's facilities were heavily dam-

Grumman Hellcat fighters of the United States Navy. One of the fastest fighters of its era, it was the first US aircraft developed from combat experience.

aged by the time the striking force turned for their carriers, which in the meantime had been successfully fending off attacks by the Army and Navy torpedo planes, by the Marine Corps scout-bombers and by Army Flying Fortresses from Midway. The four B26's and six Avengers attacked simultaneously, but achieved no hits and all but two B26's and one Avenger fell easy victims to the defending Zeros, as did many of the Dauntless and Vindicators who likewise achieved nothing. High-level bombing by the Fortresses proved no more successful against ships at sea than it had in the European theatre.

By 0830 the air striking power of Midway had expended itself, all to no concrete avail. In Nagumo's ships a feeling of elation prevailed: everywhere that is except on the Admiral's bridge where Nagumo, never the most sanguine of commanders in spite of

his record of success to date, had been in a torment of indecision brought about by a fatal flaw in the plan conceived by Yamamoto.

Precautions against the Striking Force being surprised by an enemy fleet had been taken in the shape of air reconnaissance to the eastward by seven seaplanes catapulted at dawn. Furthermore, Nagumo had withheld from his Midway strike half the Vals of the *Hiryu* and *Soryu* and half the Kates from the *Akagi* and *Kaga*, the latter armed with torpedoes. Nevertheless, should an enemy fleet be discovered before Midway had been effectively neutralised, he would find himself forced to choose between two incompatible tasks – to strike at Midway or at the enemy fleet.

This was the very situation he now found himself in. The chain of events which led to it began when, at 0700, Tomonaga, surveying the result of his attacks, signalled that there was need for a second strike. At 0715, therefore, the Kates ranged on the decks of the *Akagi* and *Kaga*, were ordered to be struck down into the hangars to exchange their torpedoes for bombs.

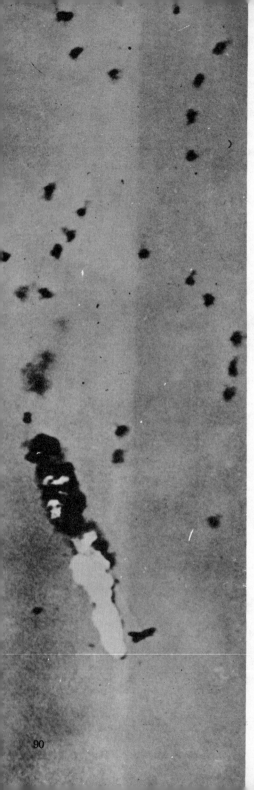

Thirteen minutes later, Nagumo's quandary was born when a signal from the seaplane from the cruiser *Tone* was handed to him, reporting a force of ten enemy ships about 300 miles to the eastward. For fifteen minutes Nagumo wrestled gloomily with the problem posed, made more difficult by the failure of the *Tone's* plane to report what types of ships had been sighted. He finally decided upon a compromise. The second strike was to prepare to attack the enemy ships, only those Kates which had not yet changed to bombs retaining their torpedoes. Meanwhile a signal demanding amplification of its report was made to the *Tone's* plane and urgently repeated ten minutes later.

Whether in the absence of any news of enemy carriers, Nagumo would have launched this strike will never be known. For the next thirty minutes it was impossible to do so; for his carriers were fully occupied, weaving this way and that to avoid the bombs of the Marine scout-bombers and the Army Fortresses from Midway, and, in the midst of it, torpedoes from the US submarine *Nautilus*. The only aircraft to take off were the Zeros ranged on deck to accompany the strike, but now thrown in to the battle raging overhead.

From that moment the strike could only be launched without fighter escort, a step which Nagumo rejected in spite of a signal at 0820 from the *Tone's* plane that the enemy was accompanied by what appeared to be a carrier and in spite of a message at 0830 from his subordinate, Rear Admiral Yamaguchi in the *Hiryu*, urging him to do so.

At this moment the returning first strike wave hove in sight. Some would be damaged, all would be low in petrol. They must be landed on at once. Nagumo gave the signal which was to decide the outcome of the Battle of Midway – to clear the carriers' decks by striking down the second wave.

For the next 45 minutes Nagumo's carrier decks were scenes of frenzied activity as planes landed on in quick

Left: A Japanese plane, flying through a hail of flak, is hit by navy gunners on a United States aircraft carrier

Douglas Dauntless. *Speed:* 275 mph. *Max range:* 464 miles. *Armament:* two
.30 machine guns, and one .5 inch machine gun. *Bomb load:* one 500 lb bomb

succession and were taken over by their ground crews for refuelling and re-arming. Down in the hangars the heavy torpedoes were being wheeled on their trolleys to the Kate bombers. In the *Kaga* and *Akagi* the bombs they replaced were simply dumped along the sides of the hangars to await a convenient moment to return them to the magazines. And while the carriers were in this most perilous and vulnerable condition, all unperceived, nemesis was winging its way towards them.

In the American carrier force, 200 miles north-east of Midway, 4th June had begun with a fly-off of a dawn search at 0430 by 10 scout planes from the *Yorktown* to the northward. They had been gone an hour when Fletcher's flagship intercepted the reports of Nagumo's carriers made by the Midway Catalinas. Here at last was the expected target. Immediately Fletcher signalled to Spruance's Task Force 16 – *Enterprise* and *Hornet* – to 'proceed south-westerly and attack enemy carriers when definitely located'. He would follow in the *Yorktown* as soon as his scouts were gathered in.

As TF16 headed away at 25 knots, Spruance's two carriers prepared to launch their striking forces. Spruance realised the opportunity presented to him of catching the enemy carriers in their most vulnerable state as they were recovering their Midway strike. He decided to throw in his entire striking strength. Not all could be ranged up and launched together. The dive-bombers – 33 from *Enterprise* led by her air group commander, Lieutenant Commander Clarence W McClusky, 35 from the *Hornet* led by Commander Stanhope C Ring – comprised the first launch. While the remainder were being ranged up and taking off they orbited overhead. But at this moment the *Tone's* scouting seaplane was sighted. The enemy would now be fully alerted. Not a moment must be wasted if his counter-attack was to be frustrated. The dive-bombers of the *Enterprise* were ordered to lead off without waiting for the torpedo planes and escort. On the assumption that Nagumo would continue to steer south-easterly, as last reported, they set course to intercept. Unsuspected by McClusky, however, or by Ring who led off with the *Hornet's* dive-bombers and fighters later, Nagumo altered course to the north-east, making their own course too far to the south.

On finding no enemy at the expected point of interception, Ring turned south with the whole of the *Hornet's* dive-bomber and fighter force. They found nothing; running short of fuel the fighters force-landed in the sea, the bombers landed on Midway or returned to their carrier direct.

Admiral Chuichi Nagumo, commander of the Japanese fleet at Midway

Had McClusky made the same decision as Ring, the outcome of the Battle of Midway might have been very different from what it was. Instead he turned to starboard, to the north-west, a choice that was to bring him fame and glory.

Meanwhile the torpedo squadrons from *Enterprise* and *Hornet* had been launched and set off to seek the enemy. Lieutenant Commander John C Waldron, commanding the *Hornet's* group of 15 torpedo planes, while taking final instructions from his Captain, Marc Mitscher, had studied the situation as laid out on the bridge plotting chart. The conviction reached him that the enemy would certainly turn to close the distance between the opposing forces. When he led off, he steered accordingly, a course which was to take him on a bee-line for his target.

Lieutenant Commander Lindsey, leading the *Enterprise's* group of 14 Devastators evidently reached a similar conclusion, though the course he steered diverged a little to the south-ward of Waldron's. High above the two torpedo squadrons, which flew low over the water, were the 10 Wildcats from the *Enterprise* led by Lieutenant James S Gray. His task was to protect Lindsey's squadron and it had been arranged that Lindsey would call him down when the torpedo planes started in to the attack.

At 0920 Waldron sighted his target ahead. Unsupported and unprotected, he went straight in to the attack. Some miles to the south of him, Lindsey saw the enemy almost simultaneously and attacked a few minutes later. For some reason, he failed to make the agreed radio call to Gray who remained circling high above while the two torpedo squadrons met catastrophe.

In the Japanese carriers, the last planes of the Midway strike had just touched down and Nagumo's ships had swung round in obedience to his signal to steer north-easterly to close the distance between him and the enemy. Fresh planes for a striking force were already being sent up on deck, the first to go up being the Zero fighters. So that when, at about 0920, reports of a swarm of enemy planes approaching were received from the ships of the outer screen, a dozen Zeros from each ship were quickly airborne. Their easy prey they found almost at once – the formation of 15 slow, defenceless Devastator torpedo planes from the *Hornet*. Within a few minutes every one had been shot into the sea, the majority before they could even release their torpedoes.

It was not time yet for exulting, however; for already Lindsey's 14 Devastators were approaching, skimming low over the water from two sides. More Zeros swooped on them sending one after the other in a burst of spray into the water. Four only escaped, their torpedoes launched hastily and blindly before they swung away out of the deadly holocaust.

Some 30 minutes of comparative quiet followed, during which Zeros were landed on to replenish ammunition for their cannons and machine guns, and immediately launched again to a storm of 'Banzais'. Hardly were they airborne when fresh targets presented themselves – 12 more Devastators winging in low over the water.

From the *Yorktown* as soon as her scouting planes returned, a strike of 12 torpedo planes led by Lieutenant Commander Lance E Massey, escorted by 6 Wildcats, as well as 17 dive-bombers led by Lieutenant Commander Maxwell F Leslie, had taken off at 0820. It was Massey's squadron that was now attacking. This time they were shepherded by the half dozen Wildcats which twisted, dived and climbed in an effort to protect the lumbering torpedo planes. They were out-numbered and outmanoeuvred by the Zeros and, though they managed to shoot down a few of the Japanese fighters, it was all in vain. One after another, the Devastators crumpled and splashed. Only two escaped. All their torpedoes were avoided.

Wild cheers broke out on board the Japanese ships at this spectacular proof of their invincibility. Preparations to launch their own striking force had been going ahead with enthusiasm and by 1024 they had been all ranged; engines were warming up; now the order for the carriers to turn into the wind to launch was given. The Zeros waiting to land on and refuel were orbiting low down.

At this moment the rising, whining scream of diving planes was heard:

the whistle of falling bombs struck sudden terror into hearts so recently exultant. Around the *Kaga*, *Akagi* and *Soryu* tall splashes of white water stained by the brown of bomb explosions rose high into the air. In the midst of them the ships lurched and shook from the shock of direct hits, plunging down through the flimsy flight decks to burst in the hangars or below, detonating bombs and torpedoes, rupturing petrol supply pipes and starting raging conflagrations. In the twinkling of an eye, triumph had been turned to disaster.

The two formations of dive-bombers from the *Enterprise* and *Yorktown* had by good fortune arrived over the *Akagi*, *Kaga* and *Soryu* almost simultaneously. (In the confused manoeuvres to avoid the torpedo attacks the *Hiryu* had become detached from the others). McCluskey, after casting to starboard in his search for the enemy, had sighted the white wake of a lone, speeding destroyer. Correctly judging that it must be steering to rejoin the main body, he had decided to follow it. The destroyer had been hunting the *Nautilus* after her earlier attack, and now unwittingly led the *Enterprise's* dive-bombers to their target.

Leslie, following Massey, had taken a more direct route; and so, as McCluskey arrived from the south-west, Leslie came in from the east. Neither were molested by defending Zeros, for they were all down low, enjoying their brief triump over the torpedo planes. Indeed the presence of neither of the dive-bomber formations was known to the Japanese until it was announced by the screaming seaward plunge of the planes.

Leslie's squadron was the first to attack. They selected the huge bulk of the *Kaga* for their target. Four direct hits reduced her in a few seconds to a flaming wreck, her bridge and flight deck destroyed, petrol gushing from fractured pipes and tanks feeding the flames.

McCluskey divided his larger force between the *Akagi* and *Soryu*. Nagumo's flagship received two bomb hits, neither of them fatally destructive in themselves, but the same deadly chain reaction of fire, burst petrol systems and gas explosions that had destroyed the *Lexington* at the Coral

Sea, tore the great ship asunder. Within a few minutes it was clear that the *Akagi* was doomed. At the urgent pleas of his staff, the Admiral abandoned her and transferred to the light cruiser *Nagara* of the screen where he could continue to exercise command.

The *Soryu*, with three direct hits, suffered the same fate. Though all three ships, burning furiously, remained afloat for some hours, the *Kaga* and *Soryu* sinking between 1900 and 1930, while the *Akagi* had to be given the *coup-de-grâce* by Japanese torpedoes ten hours later, Nagumo's

Attacking Japanese planes attempt to force their way through a heavy barrage at the Battle of Midway. *Left: The Hiryu*, last survivor in Nagumo's striking force.

Striking Force had, in the course of a few minutes been reduced to a single ship, the *Hiryu*.

There, the thrusting Yamaguchi, who had seen the fatal outcome of Nagumo's earlier vacillation, had lost not a moment in launching a strike composed of 18 dive-bomber Vals and six Zero's, led by the experienced Michio Kobayashi, a veteran of every one of the exploits of the Nagumo force. Following homeward-bound American planes, he was led to the *Yorktown*. Radar detected his formation when he was still nearly 50 miles away. Wildcats on patrol were directed on to him. One after another the Vals were sent flaming down into the sea. Only eight survived to attack the carrier, but they did so with the suicidal valour typical of the Japanese. Three were shot down by the gunfire of the *Yorktown* or her screen. But of the five who survived, three scored direct hits. From their reports on getting back to the *Hiryu*, Yamaguchi felt confident that the only enemy carrier so far located had been effectively knocked out.

The fate of the *Yorktown* might now

Map labels:
Novosibirsk
L. Baikal
Irkutsk
U S S R
Aral Sea
Ulan Bator
MANCHUKUO (MANCHURIA)
Amur
Harbin
Vladivostok
MONGOLIA
Tashkent
Urumchi
Mukden
Peking
KOREA
C H I N A
Seoul
AFGHAN-ISTAN
TIBET
Hwang Ho
Nanking
Shanghai
Indus
Delhi
NEPAL
Lhasa
Yangtse-Kiang
Chungking
Ryukyu Is.
Karachi
Ganges
Calcutta
BURMA
Mekong
Hongkong (Br.)
Okinawa
TAIWAN
OCT 23/26, 194
BATTLE OF
LEYTE GULF
INDIA
Bombay
Bay of Bengal
Rangoon
THAI-LAND
FRENCH INDO-CHINA
Hainan
LUZON
PHILIPPINE
Arabian Sea
Madras
Bangkok
Saigon
Manila
San Berna Str.
Mindoro
Leyte
Surigao
CEYLON
Trincomalee
Colombo
Sulu Sea
MINDANAO
Maldive Islands
MALAYA
SARAWAK
Brunei
Tawi Tawi
CELEBES
Equator
SUMATRA
Singapore
BORNEO
APRIL 5/9, 1942
JAP. CARRIER
AIRCRAFT RAID
CEYLON PORTS
DUTCH EAST INDIE
Batavia
JAVA
I N D I A N   O C E A N
Darwin
AUST
Mercator's Projection

have been the same as that of the Japanese carriers; for she, too, had been refuelling planes shortly before the attack. But the lessons of the Coral Sea Battle had been well absorbed. In good time the petrol system had been drained and refilled with non-inflammable CO_2 gas. For a time the ship was brought to a halt through

damage to her boiler uptakes, and Admiral Fletcher was forced to shift his flag to a cruiser. But by 1340 she was under way again, her flight decks patched and able to operate her planes.

Yamaguchi's satisfaction did not, in any case, last long. A scouting plane sent up from the *Soryu* shortly

To most men who flew her in World War II, the B-17 was "lady luck" herself...

They gave her names like Susie-Q and Rosie. But to the enemy she was a devil in the sky. You'll see why—in this gripping story of the plane and her scrappy, brave flyers . . . illustrated with hundreds of photographs. (If you were in the Air Force, many startling candid shots will have personal meaning for you.)

Flying Fortress takes you on bombing missions over Europe and the Pacific . . . on day and night-time air raids of Leipzig, Cologne, Berlin, Tokyo. You'll find out: How a personality clash almost kept the first B-17 from getting off the drawing board • Why one of the best spare parts for the B-17 was an empty tin can • What happened when the German high command marked the U.S. 100th Bomb Group for special extermination... for breaking the "gentlemen's agreement" of aerial combat • How a B-17 returned from a bombing mission in one piece—but without a pilot!

Flying Fortress illuminates the history of the air battles of the Second World War as no other
(continued on last page)

1701. History of the Second World War. Basil Liddell Hart. Every major battle on land, sea, in the air. Pub. ed. $12.50

8730. Mao Tse-Tung on Guerrilla Warfare. Transl. by Gen. Samuel B. Griffith. Communist "handbook." Pub. ed. $4.95

9126. The Frigates. James Henderson. "Dreadnaughts" of Napoleonic era. Every chase, battle. Illus. Pub. ed. $5.95

Counts As One Book

8904. Wars of America. Robert Leckie. Colonial wars to Vietnam. 2 books, counts as one. 1,000 pages. Pub. ed. $12.50

3590. Inside the Third Reich. Albert Speer. "I recommend . . . without reservations," N.Y. Times. Pub. ed. $12.50

8961. The War in the Air. The Royal Air Force in World War II. Anthology ed. by Gavin Lyall. Illus. Pub. ed. $7.95

Counts As One Book

2428. The Rising Sun. John Toland. Inside Imperial Japan. Over 60 rare photos. 2 books, counts as one. Pub. ed. $12.95

8714. The Two-Ocean War. Samuel Eliot Morison. Story of U.S. Navy in action from 1939 to V-J Day. Pub. ed. $15.00

8854. Iron Coffins. Herbert A. Werner. German U-boat captain's memoirs of submarine warfare in W.W.II. Pub. ed. $7.95

8813. Strategy, 2nd Rev. Ed. B. H. Liddell Hart. Classic book on warfare. Strategists from 490 BC to Hitler. Pub. ed. $10.00

B-17 TAIL-GUNNER
READY FOR ACTION

FLYING FORTRESS
The Illustrated Biography of the B-17s and the
Men Who Flew Them · by EDWARD JABLONSKI

EXTRA FEATURES:
■ Original Blueprint Drawings of the B-17, from wings and fuselage to engines and guns.
■ Pilot's Training Manual—how to fly the B-17. Even how to ditch it.

8755. **Flying Fortress.** Edward Jablonski. The B-17s and the men who flew them. 400 album photos. Pub. ed. $10.95

(continued from inside)

book can. Take it, if you wish, as one of your 4 introductory books, along with trial membership.

Look over the books described inside. You won't find a listing like it in any other book club. The MILITARY BOOK CLUB offers you an exciting range of books on hot wars and cold ones. Important combat biographies and revealing memoirs. Significant books on military history and international affairs. Savings are always substantial, too. On the average, 30% below publishers' edition prices, plus shipping and handling.

You're invited to try the Club on a trial-membership basis. Simply choose any 4 books (including, if you wish, *Flying Fortress*). They are worth up to $50 in the original publishers' editions. Take them all

B-17 s CROSSING THE ENGLISH CHANNEL
U.S. AIR FORCE PHOTOS

for only 98¢, plus shipping and handling. But send no money now. Examine the books for 10 days without charge and keep them only if you're delighted.

**The Military Book Club
Garden City, N.Y. 11530**

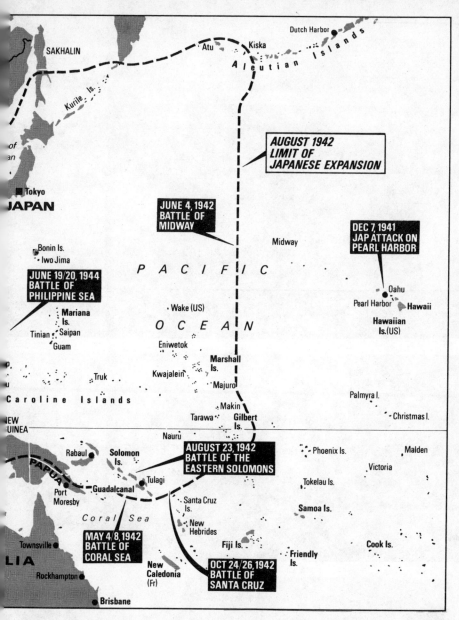

SAKHALIN

Kurile Is.

Aleutian Islands

Dutch Harbor

Atu   Kiska

of
an

■ Tokyo

JAPAN

AUGUST 1942
LIMIT OF
JAPANESE EXPANSION

JUNE 4, 1942
BATTLE OF
MIDWAY

Midway

DEC 7, 1941
JAP ATTACK ON
PEARL HARBOR

• Bonin Is.
• Iwo Jima

JUNE 19/20, 1944
BATTLE OF
PHILIPPINE SEA

P A C I F I C

Oahu
Pearl Harbor ● **Hawaii**

**Hawaiian
Is.(US)**

• Wake (US)

**Mariana
Is.**
Tinian • **Saipan**
Guam

O C E A N

Eniwetok

**Marshall
Is.**

Kwajalein •   • Majuro

Palmyra I.

• Truk

Caroline   Islands

Makin
Tarawa •••   **Gilbert
Is.**

• Christmas I.

JEW
UINEA

Nauru

Phoenix Is.

Malden

Rabaul ●   **Solomon
Is.**

AUGUST 23, 1942
BATTLE OF THE
EASTERN SOLOMONS

Victoria

PAPUA

Tulagi •

Tokelau Is.

Port
Moresby   **Guadalcanal**

Samoa Is.

Coral   Sea

• Santa Cruz
  Is.

• New
  Hebrides

Fiji Is. •••

Cook Is.

Townsville ●

MAY 4/8, 1942
BATTLE OF
CORAL SEA

**New
Caledonia
(Fr)**

OCT 24/26, 1942
BATTLE OF
SANTA CRUZ

• **Friendly
Is.**

LIA

Rockhampton ●

● **Brisbane**

before she was hit had located all
three of the American carriers. His
radio becoming defective, the pilot
had flown back and landed on the
Hiryu with the startling news. With
only ten torpedo planes and six
fighters remaining available, Yamaguchi nevertheless determined to
make a despairing effort. The daunt-

less Tomonaga, in spite of a damaged
wing tank which left him petrol
enough only for a one-way flight, led
the strike which took off at 12.45.

The *Yorktown* being the first to be
sighted, was again the target. Intercepting fighters shot down half the
force, but five Kates survived, four of
them pressing home their attacks.

The end of the *USS Yorktown. Above:* the Japanese score a direct hit on the carrier: *left* and *below left,* crew members and airmen fight the fires and attend to casualties: *below right,* survivors are transferred to a rescuing destroyer

The carrier, by this time under way again at twenty knots, swerved aside from two of the torpedoes, but two others streaking for her port side could not be avoided. Their explosions shook the great ship from stem to stern, all power was lost and she came once again to a stop, listing far over to port. Fearing that she might capsize at any moment, her captain gave the order to abandon ship. Destroyers picked up the crew and the *Yorktown* was left to die. She was not to do so for a long while yet, however; and meanwhile vengeance was to be exacted on her assailant.

At the very moment that the *Yorktown's* hull was being torn open by Tomonaga's torpedoes, one of her search planes located and reported the elusive *Hiryu*. Spruance, now in tactical command, at once ordered a strike. From the *Enterprise*, 24 dive-bombers, some of them refugees from the *Yorktown*, took off at 15.30. Thirty minutes later they were followed by sixteen more Dauntless from the *Hornet*.

On board the *Hiryu*, the last of Yamaguchi's strike planes had been re-armed, refuelled and ranged on deck for a final effort when at 17.00, unobserved from out of the sun, Lieutenant Gallaher, making his second attack of the day, led the *Enterprise* strike diving down to the attack. Four direct hits destroyed the *Hiryu's* flight deck, hurling the forward lift bodily against the island structure and setting off the fatal chain of fires and explosions that had doomed her squadron mates earlier. By the time the *Hornet's* planes arrived she was ablaze from end to end and no longer a worthwhile target. Their bombs were loosed on the battleship *Haruna* and two of the screening cruisers but failed to score any hits.

Like the other carriers hit by bombs that day, the *Hiryu* was not immediately sunk by them. The uncontrollable fires raging between decks forced her crew to abandon her at 04.30 the following morning 5th June. Torpedoes were then launched from Japanese destroyers to hasten her end; but it was not until 09.00 that she at last rolled over and sank.

So the last of Nagumo's once splendid fast carrier force perished, victim, like her sisters, of Yamamoto's faulty plan, a plan which disregarded two of the main principles of war – the maintenance of the objective and concentration of force. By assigning two incompatible aims to the Nagumo force he caused it to fail in each. By spreading his available force across the wide sea area between Midway and the Aleutians, he allowed himself to be defeated in detail.

Had he concentrated his available carrier strength, adding the *Ryujo*, the *Junyo* and the *Zuiho* to the fleet carriers and kept his tremendous battleship strength in close support, the American fleet must have been either overwhelmed or forced to retreat and abandon Midway. But his main Body with the *Zuiho* was 350 miles away to the northwest, while his other two carriers were expending their force on a subsidiary diversion in the Aleutians. Even now he hoped to retrieve the situation by bringing the American fleet to action with his battleships by night. The several scattered groups of heavy ships were ordered forward for this purpose.

Spruance had no intention of allowing himself to be so engaged, and with nightfall he withdrew eastwards reversing course again before daylight on the 5th to be in position to launch further air strikes. Realisation of the failure of his hopes came to Yamamoto during the night and with it, the acceptance of defeat. All his units were recalled, the invasion of Midway was cancelled and in deep humiliation he shaped course for Japan.

His cup of bitterness was not yet full. The four cruisers *Kumano*, *Suzuya*, *Mikuma* and *Mogami* which had been scheduled to bombard Midway, steaming through the night in obedience to the recall, encountered the American submarine *Tambor* on patrol some 90 miles west of Midway. From the flagship *Kumano* a signal for an emergency turn to port was flashed down the line. The rear ship, *Mogami*, failing to take it in, rammed the *Mikuma* ahead of her. Both were damaged and reduced in speed. The cruiser admiral, anxious to make the ordered rendezvous with his C-in-C steamed off, leaving them to limp along as best they could.

The end is near. The *Yorktown*, torn apart by Japanese bombs and torpedoes, lists to port before sinking

By daylight on 5th June all but these two of Yamamoto's major units had retired beyond the reach of Midway's scouting Catalinas. It was on them, therefore, that American bombing efforts were concentrated. Army bombers failed to find them; but twelve surviving Marine dive-bombers from the island attacked them that morning. No bomb hits were achieved; but Captain Richard E Fleming, hit by gunfire at the point of release, with selfless valour crashed his Vindicator on to the *Mikuma's* after turret, further damaging her and starting fires.

By the afternoon Spruance's carriers were within striking range; but a force of 58 dive-bombers failed to find the cruisers. Early on the 6th, however, his scouting planes located them and a massive strike was soon on its way. Both ships were heavily hit. The *Mikuma* went to the bottom, but the *Mogami* incredibly stayed afloat, a tangled wreck, and eventually worked her way to the Japanese island base of Truk in the Carolines.

The Battle of Midway was over – a crushing defeat of the Japanese fleet by a force vastly inferior in numbers, almost unimaginable unless the new form that naval warfare had taken was appreciated. Only the carrier now really counted, just as Admiral Sims had predicted 19 years before.

Complete as the American victory was, one final episode being played out was to mar its perfection. The *Yorktown*, abandoned on the afternoon of the 4th, listing heavily, had stayed afloat on the calm sea for the rest of the day and through the following night. Then destroyers standing by her suggested she was salvable. A minesweeper took her in tow; a salvage party from her crew was taken back on board by her Captain; by the afternoon of 6th June with the destroyer *Hamman* alongside to provide water and electric power and other destroyers circling to form an anti-submarine screen, she was making slow progress towards Pearl Harbor. She was never to reach it, however. The Japanese submarine, *I.168* located her and, taken skilfully through the screen, fired four torpedoes, one of which hit and sank the *Hamman*, two others exploding against the carrier's starboard side. Once again the *Yorktown* was abandoned as the sea cascaded into her riven hull. Yet even now the ill-used ship refused to succumb to her many wounds for another twelve hours. But at last, early on the 7th, the *Yorktown's* end came as she rolled slowly over to port and plunged to the bottom.

Carriers turn the tide in the Pacific

With one astonishing blow, the Battle of Midway wiped out the hitherto overwhelming Japanese carrier superiority. Three American carriers repulsed and inflicted tremendous losses on virtually the whole naval strength of the Empire. By doing so, they destroyed any Japanese hopes of expanding their perimeter eastward.

In the South Pacific, the halt called by the Coral Sea Battle had been a temporary one only. The seaborne expedition to capture Port Moresby had been replaced by a land campaign launched from Japanese bases on the north coast of Papua. Australian and other Allied forces of General Douglas MacArthur's South-West Pacific Command met and were ultimately to repel this thrust.

Meanwhile the prosecution of Japanese strategy, whether to advance to cut Allied oceanic communications between Pearl Harbour and the South Pacific, or simply to consolidate the vast conquests so rapidly made, was to come to depend upon the possession of a hitherto almost unheard-of and almost uninhabitable island of the Solomons, the swampy,

fever-infested Guadalcanal. Unattractive as this island was from almost every point of view, it had one feature which made it a vital bone of contention. Unlike its neighbours, it had an area of level ground running along its north shore on which an airfield could be constructed. Soon after the Japanese set up their seaplane base at Tulagi, they sent a labour battalion to Guadalcanal to construct a landing strip. When Allied air reconnaissance discovered this going on, it was at once clear that possession of the island was the key to the control of the South Western Pacific. The capture and retention of the airfield site was assigned as the primary and most urgent task of Admiral Ghormley's South Pacific Command. It would depend ultimately upon control of the adjacent sea areas through which the land forces, contending ashore for mastery, must be supplied.

This, in turn, revolved round air power and, in the absence of land air bases, on naval air power. It was fortunate, therefore, that CINCPAC, Admiral Nimitz, as a result of Midway, was able to send three of his four

Admiral Nimitz, C in C Pacific

carriers, *Enterprise, Saratoga* (newly joined after repairs) and *Wasp* (transferred from the Atlantic) to join the South Pacific Command, the carrier force being commanded by Vice Admiral Frank Fletcher with his flag in the 'Sara'.

When the Allied invasion fleet arrived off Guadalcanal on 7th August 1942 it was from these mobile airfields, stationed close by, that a swarm of Wildcats were able to meet and defeat the Japanese bombers sent from Rabaul, the nearest air-base, some 560 nautical miles away. The mass of bulky transports escaped almost unscathed to land 17,000 US Marines and capture the almost completed airstrip, henceforth named Henderson Field after a Marine air hero of Midway. Marine dive-bombers and fighters were soon established there.

Both sides now strove to run reinforcements through to their forces on Guadalcanal. The Japanese relied for this principally upon fast night runs by destroyers – the 'Tokyo Express' as it came to be called by the Americans. But Admiral Yamamoto, still seeking to bring about a naval battle in which his greatly superior strength in battleships and heavy cruisers could be brought into play, brought his Combined Fleet south to Truk whence, on 21st August, it sortied to cover a small force of transports from Rabaul escorted by the destroyers of the 'Tokyo Express' and a squadron of four heavy cruisers.

Yamamoto's plan was typically complex with the same dispersal of force which had proved so fatal at Midway. Following a broad scouting line of submarines, was an Advance Force of six cruisers and the seaplane carrier *Chitose* under Vice Admiral Kondo to scout far in advance of a Vanguard Group composed of two battleships and three cruisers. Under cover of this operated the Striking Force, the carriers *Zuikaku* and *Shokaku*, the latter flying the flag of Nagumo, athirst to avenge Midway and recover lost 'face'. Yet another group, again a typically Japanese concept, was the sacrificial decoy or Diversionary Group centred on the

USS Saratoga off Guadalcanal. Her dive-bombers sank the little *Ryujo*

USS Enterprise. Attacked by Nagumo's strike force, her Grumman Wildcat fighters kept the 'Kate' torpedo planes at bay

little carrier *Ryujo*.

Japanese intentions were broadly known to the American command; not in detail, but enough to bring Fletcher's Task Force 61 to the eastern approaches to the Coral Sea by 21st August, whence daily searches were flown by the planes of the three carriers. They discovered and attacked two of the advancing Japanese submarines early on the 23rd; but it was seaplanes of the shore-based naval air command which located the first surface units, the troop convoy.

From the *Saratoga* and from Henderson Field, strike forces set out; but in rain and low cloud they failed to find their quarry which, in fact, had temporarily reversed course

as soon as it knew it was detected. With dusk coming on, the whole force returned to Henderson Field for the night, the Sara's planes rejoining her the next morning.

Meanwhile Fletcher, misreading the significance of the seaplane report, had decided to detach the *Wasp* to refuel at a rendezvous 240 miles to the south; so when the Japanese fleet resumed its southerly advance during the night, events were moving towards an encounter which was to find him with a third of his force absent.

It was again a seaplane which brought first news of the enemy on the morning of the 24th, reporting a carrier group some 300 miles to the northward. Fletcher initially showed more caution than he had at the Coral

Grumman F4F-3 – the 'Wildcat'. The American fighter which contributed most to the tilting of power in the Pacific. *Speed:* 331 mph. *Max range:* 860 miles. *Armament:* four .5 inch cannon

Sea. Mistrusting the report, which in fact was of the *Ryujo* which had been detached from the Japanese main body partly to play her role as a decoy and partly to launch a bombing attack on Henderson Field, he launched only an armed reconnaissance of 29 bombers and torpedo planes. But when his radar detected the *Ryujo's* strike formation some 100 miles to the westward heading for Henderson Field (where they were to meet a sharp defeat at the hands of the Marines) he accepted this as sufficient evidence on which to launch a further strike of 30 dive-bombers and eight of the new Grumman Avenger torpedo planes.

As at the Coral Sea, he had now launched the majority of his striking strength without certain knowledge of the location of their primary target - the enemy carriers. When the widespread *Enterprise* scouting planes found them, the *Saratoga's* were well on their way and could not be raised on the radio to re-direct them. The latter duly found the little *Ryujo*, the doomed scapegoat; several hits from the plummeting dive-bombers and a single torpedo hit sent her to the bottom. Of the more vital targets, only the *Shokaku* was attacked, piecemeal, by *Enterprise* scout bombers and escaped serious damage.

It was fortunate that Fletcher had profited from earlier experience in one respect. He had retained his fighter strength; so that when the massed striking force from Nagumo's carriers arrived to concentrate on the *Enterprise* they were met by more than 50 Wildcats. Even so, fighter control was far from effective at that time. Radar screens cluttered with returning friendly aircraft and anti-submarine patrols combined with a swamping of the radio channel by the excited chatter of pilots as they went into action made direction impossible.

The low-flying Japanese torpedo planes were overwhelmed and not one broke through the defences; but up at 18,000 feet the Vals were left undisturbed to go into their attacking dives. Although they were met by a seemingly impenetrable stream of gunfire, particularly from the lavish AA armament with which the new battleship *North Carolina* had been equipped, and though this destroyed a number of them, enough survived long enough to score three direct hits on the *Enterprise*, the bombs plunging through the unarmoured flight-deck to burst below and start fires.

Yet within one hour the *Enterprise* had mastered the fires patched up her flight deck and was steaming at 24 knots to recover her planes – a credit to the technical improvements made to lessen the fire hazard and to the constant practice in damage control which now paid off so handsomely.

One more clash between the rival carrier forces, the Battle of the Eastern Solomons, was over, Task Force 61 retiring southwards to refuel meet the *Wasp*, and to seek repairs for the *Enterprise*, while Nagumo, though his ships were still unharmed, had lost so many planes and pilots that he, too, could do nothing else but retire to obtain replacements – replacements which were every day becoming less well-trained and fewer in number. The Japanese troop convoy, the ostensible cause of this latest encounter, left to press on unsupported, was set upon by the aircraft from Henderson Field and by US Army bombers. After suffering casualties it was forced to retire and await a further opportunity.

The first round of the battle for Guadalcanal had been fought. There were to be numerous bloody encoun-

on which all depended. A lack of prudent precautions in the face of a submarine threat deployed by the Japanese came near to eliminating it.

To replace the *Enterprise*, under repair at Pearl Harbor, had come the *Hornet*. The area in which flying operations were carried out remained much the same, day after day; so that when the *Saratoga's* group, in company with that of the *Hornet*, was patrolling at the moderate speed of 13 knots on 31st August, the Japanese submarine *I-26* had no difficulty in ambushing them and torpedoing the *Saratoga*.

Above and right: The end of the *Wasp,* September 15th 1942. Three torpedoes from Japanese submarine 1-19 tore a gash in her hull and fractured pipe-lines which then leaked fuel. A spark ignited the vapour and a series of explosions wrecked the ship which had to be abandoned and sunk

ters between the surface forces on either side, always at night, in which the Japanese displayed their superior skill and training and time and again had the better of the exchange in spite of their lack of radar. By day, however, control of the waters round Guadalcanal belonged to the side with air superiority. The capacity of Henderson Field, limited always, was repeatedly crippled by heavy naval bombardments by night. It was the carrier force of the South Pacific Command, therefore, operating in the eastern approaches of the Coral Sea,

Fortunately only one torpedo hit her and she was able to limp away for repairs at Pearl Harbor.

American carrier strength was now down to two. Six days later the *Hornet* was narrowly missed by torpedoes from the Japanese submarine *I-II*. By this time the area had been dubbed 'Torpedo Junction' by American sailors; but the implications had not been absorbed, it seems; for on 15th September the *I-19* found the Task Force operating in the same general area and was able to put three torpedoes into the *Wasp*, as a result of which she had to be abandoned and sunk. At about the same time the battleship *North Carolina* and a destroyer on the screen of the *Hornet's* group, were also both torpedoed and damaged by the same submarine or by *I-15* which was also operating near by.

With the situation approaching the desperate, Nimitz had the repairs to the *Enterprise* rushed through and on 16th October she sailed for the South Pacific with the new battleship *South Dakota* and a reinforcement of nine destroyers. Under the command of Rear Admiral Thomas C Kinkaid,

American carriers were opposed by the *Shokaku* and *Zuikaku*, the two smaller *Junyo* and *Hiyo*, the latter a sister ship of the *Junyo* which was about to join the fleet, and the little *Zuiho*. But no additions to the Japanese carrier fleet could be expected until the end of 1943 when the conversion of two passenger liners would be completed.

Such was the situation when, with the critical phase of the struggle on land for Guadalcanal in progress, Yamamoto sent the whole Combined Fleet south to the area north of the Santa Cruz Islands in support on

they were designated Task Force 16. The bottom of the barrel had been scraped. The *Saratoga* could not complete repairs until the end of November.

A brighter situation was soon to arrive with the commissioning of the *Essex* at the end of the year, the first of a class of eleven similar ships of 27,100 tons capable of operating 110 aircraft, and of the 11,000 ton light carrier *Independence*, in January 1943, first of ten converted from light cruisers, each of which could operate 35 aircraft. In the meantime the two

22nd October. Under the supreme command of Vice Admiral Kondo, it was, as usual, divided into several widely separated forces. Kondo himself, with his flag in the heavy cruiser *Atago*, remained with the so-called Advance Force, comprising four cruisers, two battleships and destroyer screen, and the carrier *Junyo* which manoeuvred separately with her own screen. Some 120 miles to the southeastward was the Striking Force, the carriers *Shokaku* (flagship of Vice Admiral Nagumo) *Zuikaku* and *Zuiho* with the usual destroyer screen.

Sixty miles to the southward of Nagumo, was the Vanguard Force of two battleships, three heavy cruisers and destroyer screen.

The new Commander South Pacific, the thrusting Vice Admiral 'Bill' Halsey, was not disposed to allow this to go unchallenged and, as soon as Task Force 16 arrived, it was ordered to join the *Hornet* group, Task Force 17, off the Santa Cruz Islands. Rendezvous was made on the 24th when Kinkaid assumed command of the whole force and, in accordance with his orders, took it northwards on a sweep round the islands.

Nagumo's force was located by scouting Catalinas on the 25th but by the time a carrier search and strike force had been launched the Japanese had turned away to the north and evaded them. The Japanese carriers were again reported and unsuccessfully attacked by Army bombers and by torpedo carrying Catalinas during the night. Kinkaid had the carrier man's mistrust of the accuracy of long-range shore-based reconnaissance, however, and he had no doubt studied the results of Fletcher's impetuosity on earlier occasions. It was a searching force of his own, comprising eight pairs of Dauntless scout bombers, which fanned out from the *Enterprise* at dawn on the 26th.

Even when a typically terse message from Halsey reached him at about the same time, 'Attack – repeat – Attack', it was not until a pair of his scouts reported Nagumo at 06.50, less than 200 miles to the north-west, that he ordered a strike to be launched. At 07.30, from the *Hornet*, 15 dive-bombers, 6 Avenger torpedo planes and eight Wildcats set off without waiting for the *Enterprise* strike of 3 dive-bombers, 8 Avengers and 8 Wildcats which took off half-an-hour later. A second strike formation from the *Hornet* followed at 08.15, composed of nine Dauntless, 9 Avengers and 9 fighters.

Nagumo received confirmation of his opponent's position almost simultaneously with Kinkaid. He was quicker off the mark, however, and by 07.00 a striking force of 65 planes, about half of them escorting Zeros, had taken off from his three carriers. Hardly had they done so when, out of the broken clouds above, two

Dauntless screamed down to put their 500lb bombs squarely on the *Zuiho's* flight deck, punching a huge jagged hole and setting her ablaze, which put her out of action for further flying operations. Lieutenant Commander S B Strong and Ensign C B Irvine, piloting a pair of scouts from the *Enterprise's* dawn search, had made clever use of the clouds to evade the Zeros on defensive patrol and arrive undetected and unopposed.

Meanwhile the opposing strike formations were winging their way towards their respective targets. The American force, strung out in three separate groups, and the compact Japanese strike, sighted each other on opposite courses. From the swarm of Zeros accompanying the latter, a dozen detached and, coming in out of the sun, pounced on the *Enterprise* group, shooting down four Avengers and four Wildcats at the cost of three of their own number.

Both carrier forces were thus warned of the approaching storm and sent their defending fighters aloft in good time. In Kinkaid's force operating in two separate groups some ten miles apart, the up-to-date radar set in the *Enterprise* should have given the defence a clear advantage; but the fighter direction experience necessary was lacking and control only minimal. Contrary to what happened on the previous occasion, it was the Japanese dive-bombers which were intercepted, while the Kate torpedo planes swept in low, unopposed until they met the ships' gunfire, and even the Vals were engaged too late to take the sting out of the attack delivered with all the dedicated courage typical of the Japanese. At the critical moment a rain squall swept over the *Enterprise* leaving the *Hornet* to take the full weight of the attack. More than half the Kates were shot down before reaching the launching position, but the remainder pressed on to score two torpedo hits on the *Hornet's* starboard side, while a third doomed and flaming Kate crashed suicidally into the carrier's bow, exploding near the forward elevator. In a perfectly co-ordinated attack the Vals which fought their way through the fighter defence, dived from 17,000 feet. Few escaped the storm of gunfire that met them; but before crashing into the sea, three of them succeeded in releasing their 500lb bombs to achieve hits, one bursting on impact, the other two plunging through several decks before exploding; the squadron commander, fatally hit, dived his plane into the *Hornet's* superstructure. Wrecking the signal bridge, it crashed through the deck and exploded to set a furious fire blazing. Within ten devastating minutes the carrier had been reduced to a motionless, burning wreck. Very few Japanese airmen escaped to boast of their success, however.

By this time the American striking force was arriving over the widespread Japanese fleet. Setting out piecemeal, they had become further scattered *en route*. All but the 15 dive-bombers of the first strike from the *Hornet*, led by the air group commander, Lieutenant Commander Widhelm, with four escorting Wildcats succeeded only in finding the Japanese Vanguard Group which they attacked. The Avengers, still handicapped by indifferent torpedoes, achieved nothing; a *Hornet* dive-bomber of the second strike hit and heavily damaged the cruiser *Chikuma*.

It was left to Widhelm's formation to save the day. Losing his meagre fighter escort when they became engaged with Zeros sent up from the *Junyo*, he pressed on to be rewarded with the sight of the *Shokaku* and the still burning *Zuiho*. Zeros pounced; Widhelm himself was forced down into the sea[1]; another Dauntless was shot down and two turned back damaged; but the remainder, led by Lieutenant J E Vose, arrived over the *Shokaku* to dive down through the fierce barrage

and score four hits with 1,000lb bombs. The *Shokaku's* flight deck was reduced to a tangle of twisted steel; her hangar was wrecked and set on fire; her speed fell away to 21 knots. In company with *Zuiho* she limped away to be out of action for nine crucial months.

At this stage, honours might have been considered even in the Battle of the Santa Cruz Islands, though the Japanese had suffered terrible losses in men and machines to achieve the crippling of the *Hornet*. But the Americans had for the time being shot their bolt so far as strike power was concerned, whereas the second strike of 44 planes from the *Shokaku* and *Zuikaku* which had taken off at 08.22 and a further force of 29 planes from the *Junyo* were still to be brought into play.

The dive-bombers of the former arrived over the *Enterprise* at the very moment that a torpedo attack by the submarine *I-21* was being avoided and was distracting attention and, though they were met by massed gunfire from the carrier and her screen, including the *South Dakota*, which accounted for all but a handful, they scored two bomb hits. Fortunately the damage they did to the flight deck was repairable, except for the forward elevator put out of action; the carrier's speed and manoeuvrability were not affected. So when the Japanese Kates came belatedly into action, the *Enterprise* was able to avoid all their torpedoes.

Nevertheless, the carrier's crew were still struggling to repair her decks to enable her to recover the swarm of planes orbiting with rapidly emptying fuel tanks, when the *Junyo's*

The end of the *Hornet*. Flames and smoke billow from the signal bridge as the Japanese squadron commander crashes his aircraft in a suicide attack

strike suddenly swooped out of the cloud cover. Twenty of them attacked the *Enterprise*; but they were not of the calibre of the veteran carrier crews and they failed to score any hits. Others which attacked the screen, however, planted a bomb on the *South Dakota* and another on the light cruiser *San Juan*. The armoured bulk of the former saved her from damage, while, paradoxically, it was the total lack of armour of the cruiser that saved her, the armour-piercing bomb passing clean through her before exploding.

The *Enterprise* was now able to recover her waiting planes. But Kinkaid's air power, offensive and defensive, had been eliminated. Not so the Japanese, as was made clear when six enemy torpedo planes streaked in low over the water to attack the *Hornet* which had been taken in tow by the cruiser *Northampton*. One torpedo hit the carrier, finally dashing the last hopes of saving her. While preparations for abandoning her were being made, she was twice more hit by dive-bombs. These attacks all came from the *Junyo*.

Yet the gallant ship lingered. Torpedoes from American destroyers and a cannonade by 5in guns left her still floating to be finally given the *coup de grâce* by Japanese torpedoes during the night, after the American fleet had retired.

Viewed purely as a sea battle, the Santa Cruz Islands had been even more a tactical victory for the superior Japanese fleet than had been the Eastern Solomons. The Japanese were left 'in possession of the field'; the only operational carriers remaining in the Pacific all flew the Rising Sun flag – the *Zuikaku*, *Junyo* and *Hiyo*; domination of the sea approaches to Guadalcanal and the fate of the island itself might have been thought to be in their hands. In fact it was not so. The slaughter inflicted on the Japanese carrier aircrews had left only sufficient to equip the two smaller carriers which could operate less than 100 planes between them.

American possession of Henderson Field more than offset the Japanese carrier advantage. By 12th November, the *Enterprise*, temporarily repaired at Nouméa, was also once again

Above: Rear Admiral Thomas C. Kinkaid, commanding Task Force 16 at the Battle of Santa Cruz. *Right: USS Enterprise* under attack off Santa Cruz . . but the highly-skilled veterans of the Japanese days of triumph were dead, and the new, inexperienced pilots failed to score hits

operational and playing her part in the domination of the Guadalcanal area by day, leaving the opposing surface forces to fight a series of bloody night battles in which fortunes swayed to and fro, and which in the end were to force the Japanese to give up their attempts to supply their dwindling forces on the island.

Though these battles were often inconclusive or even favourable to the Japanese, daylight exposed them, as they retired, to devastating air attacks in which the *Enterprise* planes played the major part. Thus, on the morning of 13th November, after a night of battle disastrous to the Americans, it was her torpedo planes

which caught and immobilised the damaged battleship *Hiei* leaving her to be scuttled by her own crew. On the following day, after a Japanese cruiser squadron had bombarded the airfield during the night, strike planes from Guadalcanal and from the *Enterprise* combined to sink the cruiser *Kinugasa* and damage three others.

Then a large Japanese supply convoy of 11 ships and escort heading for Guadalcanal was discovered and throughout the day was pounded by naval planes leaving only four ships afloat when the sun went down. While another furious night battle off the island, in which the Americans snatched an eleventh hour victory out of defeat by benefit of radar-controlled gunfire, was taking place, the four transports beached themselves to throw-their supplies ashore, only to be destroyed by naval planes at first light.

These battles sealed the fate of Guadalcanal though it was not until the following month that the stub-born Japanese admitted defeat and took steps to evacuate their surviving forces. The war in the South West Pacific now took the shape of an Allied advance from island to island up the chain of the Solomons and the Bismarck Archipelago and onward towards the recovery of the Philippines. In this form of warfare there was little scope and unacceptable risks for carrier forces. American carrier strength, however, was now starting on a programme of spectacular expansion. With so splendid a new weapon in their hands, the Joint Chiefs of Staffs found themselves in a position to initiate a new strategy, striking at the heart of the Japanese defence system in the Central Pacific, instead of relying on the slow advance through the peripheral islands.

Before this was to get fully under way, however, a new page in the story of the aircraft carrier had been written in the European theatre where we must now return.

And in the Atlantic

At almost the same time that the tide of fortune in the Pacific War was seen to have turned with the final ejection of the Japanese from Guadalcanal, largely as a result of American carrier operations, on the other side of the world carriers were similarly playing a vital part in two other turning points of the war. The first of these was the decisive defeat of the Axis armies at the Battle of Alamein on 23rd October, 1942, in which the major factor was the great inferiority in men, munitions and fuel forced on Field-Marshal Rommel, the German commander, by the cutting of his supply routes, air and sea, across the Mediterranean. In this, the beleaguered fortress of Malta played a vital part, a part which, but for the desperate operations to fight supply ships through to her, she would have been forced to abandon.

The first of these operations was given the code-name 'Harpoon'. A convoy of six large merchant ships with a close escort of an AA cruiser, nine destroyers, and four mine-sweepers was to be given support during the passage from Gibraltar to

the Sicilian Narrows by an old battle-ship, three cruisers, eight destroyers and the veteran carriers *Eagle* and *Argus* (their combined age was no less than 47 years). The valuable major units of the fleet could not be risked inside the Narrows as the fate of the *Illustrious* had demonstrated; and since the loss of the *Ark Royal* to a U-boat attack in November 1941, even the old carriers were pearls without price as their employment on such an important operation shows.

As usual with such operations, therefore, it was so arranged that the convoy and close escort would reach the entrance to the Narrows at dusk on 14th June, 1942, when the support force would turn back for Gibraltar. Thereafter, for the final 24 hours of the voyage, the convoy would have to depend upon its close escort for defence and, after first light, on such air cover as Malta could provide.

Nevertheless, if the convoy could be safely brought to the entrance of the Narrows, half its most dangerous period would be over. It was through the long hours of daylight of 14th June that the carrier-borne fighters

112

Aircraft carrier and battleship units in the escort force for Operation Torch, the Allied invasion of North Africa

would have the task of fending off the enemy strike planes shuttling to and from Sardinian and Sicilian airfields. Making their first appearance in action were 16 of the new Sea Hurricanes on board the *Eagle*, adaptations of the obsolescent land-based Hurricane, with which the Fleet Air Arm had to make do until something better came along. They were at least of superior performance to the two-seater Fulmars, six of which were also divided between the two carriers; against the possibility of Italian surface forces threatening the convoy, and, to provide anti-submarine patrols, a force of 18 Swordfish torpedo planes was embarked in the *Argus*.

When 14th June dawned, a cloudless, blue day with the lightest of breezes from astern of the eastward steering ships, all hands braced themselves for a day of intensive action. They were not to be disappointed, though it was not until 10.00 that the first alarm came from the radar operators. Fighters from the *Eagle* were already patrolling and scored their first success by shooting down one of a forma-

tion of Italian Savoia torpedo planes gathering for an attack. From this time onwards until 21.00 that evening attack followed attack almost without pause.

From the small force of fighters, the maximum effort found practicable to keep in the air at any one time was four, occasionally six Hurricanes, which operated from the *Eagle* and concentrated on providing high cover, and two Fulmars from the *Argus* to take care of low-flying torpedo planes. Throughout the forenoon and afternoon attacks came from Italian fighter-bombers, torpedo-planes and high-level bombers, escorted by fighters. Six of them were shot down by the fighters, others by ships' gunfire. Three Hurricanes were lost, one being shot down by 'friendly' gunfire. None of the bombs did any damage; but the massed torpedo attacks could not all be avoided. The cruiser *Liverpool* was hit and forced to return to Gibraltar in tow of a destroyer where she successfully arrived in spite of a number of further bomb and torpedo attacks on her. A freighter in the convoy was sunk.

Nevertheless, as the evening approached, the convoy and its escort could feel well satisfied with their achievements. They were now coming within range of Sicilian airfields, however, and at 18.20 the German Junker 88's arrived to concentrate their attacks on the carriers; but harrassed by the Hurricanes and Fulmars, they achieved nothing better than near misses. Then came a coordinated massed attack by Italian torpedo planes, Junker 88's and Stukas. Out of the bedlam of gunfire, exploding bombs and the scream and roar of diving planes, three enemy aircraft and three British fighters were lost; but not a torpedo or a bomb found its mark. This was the last attack of the day, during which 11 enemy aircraft had been shot down by the Hurricanes and Fulmars, many others being damaged or driven off, while ship gunfire had accounted for eight. As darkness fell, the convoy and its close escort parted company from the support force and steamed on to face another day of stirring events in which an Italian cruiser force came to add its threat to that of the Italian and German aircraft. Though fighter aircraft from Malta came out to give cover, it could not be as continuous as that provided by the carriers. German dive-bombers broke through to sink three more of the merchant ships. Only two reached Malta; but they were just enough to keep the fortress going for another two vital months.

Nevertheless by August 1942 the island fortress was once again at the end of its endurance. Without supplies it would be starved into surrender. Yet again a convoy was gathered for another desperate attempt to get through to her, 13 freighters and the tanker Ohio, which passed through the Straits of Gibraltar in the early hours of 10th August, 1942. The Italian Naval Staff was well apprised of the forthcoming operation and were determined the convoy should not reach Malta. On the airfields of Sardinia and Sicily a huge fleet of 784 German and Italian bombers, dive-bombers and torpedo planes had been assembled, as well as a large number of scouting aircraft. In addition, nine submarines had been stationed between Majorca and Algiers athwart the route to Malta; 11 more waited at the entrance to the Narrows, where 23 MTB's were also to attack during the night. Finally a surface force of cruisers and destroyers was assembled to intercept the convoy in the Sicilian Channel.

The British had scraped together every ship that could be made available. The two modern carriers Victorious and Indomitable joined the hard-worked old Eagle as the air component of the supporting force, which included two battleships, Nelson and Rodney, three AA cruisers and 20 destroyers. A further force of three cruisers, one AA ship and 13 destroyers was to escort the convoy for the last 24 hours, between the entrance to the Narrows and Malta. With the convoy, too, for the first two days, would go the old Furious, loaded with 38 Spitfires to be flown off to join the defences of Malta, the latest of many similar runs by carriers with air reinforcements for the island.

Passage of the convoy through the Straits was known at once to the enemy. Early on 11th August, when south of Majorca, it was brought under air surveillance which fighters from the carriers tried in vain to shake off, the Junkers 88's being used for shadowing proving too fast for them. It was early on the same day that the force suffered a first cruel blow. The enemy submarine patrol line had been well placed and the German U 73 found herself squarely in the path of the carrier force. Four torpedoes hit the Eagle to send the veteran ship to the bottom in eight minutes with 200 of her crew.

The fighter defences were now reduced to the 6 Hurricanes and 16 Fulmars on board the Victorious, 10 Martlets (the British name for the Wildcat), and 24 Hurricanes in the Indomitable. They were able to take no part when the only air attack on that day developed as it was skilfully timed to arrive as dusk settled down, in which the fighters failed to find them. Its delivery was less skilful, however, and no ships were damaged by the 36 German bombers and torpedo planes which attacked, and which lost three of their number to ships' gunfire.

This was a heartening start to the great air battle to come. But by dawn only 70 miles would separate the ships from the Sardinian airfields when massive attacks could be expected. The 12th August was, indeed, to be an action-packed day. In the early dawn the first fighters were flown off and quickly disposed of two Italian shadowing planes. Two hours later they intercepted the first attackers, some 20 Junker 88's; the waiting watchers in the fleet were cheered by the sight of twin-engined planes spiralling down to crash in the sea or breaking away, jettisoning their bombs, with fighters in pursuit. The attack failed; six German aircraft were shot down.

At mid-day came a much more ambitious effort, a co-ordinated attack by more than 100 aircraft – torpedo planes, high-level bombers, fighter bombers and dive-bombers. Some of the Italian bombers loosed a newly-devised weapon, the *motobomba*, a torpedo which, after floating down by parachute, set off on a zig-zag or circular course. From an Italian seaplane, a bomb-loaded unmanned

aircraft was radio-controlled to dive on its target. Fortunately its control failed to function and it flew away to North Africa where it crashed.

Although the *Victorious* had a lucky escape when a bomb from an Italian fighter-bomber on her flight deck failed to explode, it was a formation of German dive-bombers that achieved the only success. Met by defending fighters as they flew in to attack the convoy, only 11 managed to break through; but, concentrating on one of the freighters, they sent one bomb clean through her hull to explode beneath her, while near misses so shook her that she was temporarily brought to a halt. Left on her own, she got under way again but was discovered that evening by two torpedo-planes which sank her.

That afternoon, while the convoy passed through the submarine ambush waiting for it, sinking one Italian U-boat and damaging another in the process, minor air attacks were successfully fended off. But with the evening the convoy arrived within range of the Sicilian airfields and of the deadly Stuka dive-bombers. And

115

at 18.30 hours they arrived, accompanied by Junker 88's and Savoia torpedo-planes with a swarm of escorting fighters.

Hurricanes, Fulmars and Martlets tore into them, shooting down seven; the torpedo planes launched their torpedoes hastily and at long range, their only victim being a destroyer on the screen; but the bombers were in too great strength to be stopped entirely; a formation of Stukas and Junkers 88's concentrated on the *Indomitable* and scored three hits. Her armoured flight deck was not penetrated but it was badly damaged and put out of action, her fighters having to land on the *Victorious*.

The time had now come for the supporting force and carriers to part company with the convoy and close escort. Except for the loss of one freighter, they had successfully fought the convoy through a long day of almost continuous and massive air attack. More than 30 enemy aircraft had been shot down by the little force of obsolescent fighters at a cost to themselves of 13. The carriers could do no more, as they could not be risked in the narrow waters of the Sicilian Channel exposed to such a huge weight of enemy air attack as could be mounted from the airfields close at hand.

The convoy and close escort steamed on into the dusk. A fearful ordeal was ahead of them. Assaulted during the night by submarines, MTB's, bombers and torpedo planes and by massed air attacks the following day they suffered heavy losses. Of the escort, the cruiser *Manchester* and the AA ship *Cairo* were sunk, the cruisers *Nigeria* and *Kenya* were torpedoed and damaged. Only five ships of the convoy, three of them damaged, including the vital tanker *Ohio*, reached Malta. But they were enough, by the narrowest of margins, to keep Malta going until relief in November after the Battle of Alamein. The heavy losses to enemy aircraft during the final day of the convoy's passage made it clear that none would have got through but for the defence put up by the carriers during 12th August.

The other decisive turning point in which carriers were playing a vital rôle at this time was the victory over

Service in northern waters: *left:* the escort carriers *Emperor* and *Striker* take a pounding in heavy seas: *above:* the warships *Duke of York, Formidable,* and *Indefatigable* cruising with an aircraft carrier off the Norwegian coast

the German U-boats in the Battle of the Atlantic. They were not the fast, lavishly-equipped mobile airfields which operated with the fleets, substituting the striking power of their bombers for that of the battleships' great guns: they were the small utility carriers, converted initially from merchant ships and with a primarily defensive rôle, which were finally designated escort carriers.

The British and Americans conceived the idea of such ships at much the same time. The British *Audacity,* which had simply a flight deck superimposed on a captured German merchant ship and no elevator or hangar, was the first to see service in June 1941. Intended to give fighter protection against the German long-range aircraft attacking convoys, she carried six Martlets; but during operations with the four convoys on the

UK-Gibraltar route which she escorted in her all-too-short career, her aircraft proved equally valuable in the A/S rôle. In the fourth of these operations she played an important part in a notable defeat of the U-boats on a homeward-bound convoy in December 1941 in which four submarines were sunk, two enemy aircraft shot down, and three driven off damaged for the loss of two ships of the convoy.

Unfortunately the *Audacity* was also lost to a U-boat's torpedo, but the value of her type of ship had been impressively demonstrated. Conversion of other ships was decided upon. Meanwhile in the United States a more elaborate type of auxiliary carrier had been under conversion from a merchant ship which emerged as the *Long Island,* a ship of 7,886 tons, diesel-driven at 16 knots, which was given a flight deck and a hangar connected by a single elevator. Some 20 aircraft could be operated from her. A large programme of such ships was put in hand in the States, initially similar conversions from freighters or tankers but, as the demand grew, built-for-the-purpose ships using prefabrica-

The Fairey 'Barracuda'. *Speed:* 264 mph. *Max range:* 1,200 miles.
Armament: one .5 inch cannon. *Bomb load:* 18 inch torpedo or 2,000 lb bomb

Rocket assisted take-off by a Barracuda from the deck of the carrier *Trumpeter*

tion and 'production-line' techniques were built. The first 50 of these were of the Casablanca class, and were followed by the 'ultimate' improved design of the Commencement Bay class.

It is with the earliest of these variations, the converted merchant ships, that we are concerned here. Following the Audacity's success, the British had selected five merchantmen under construction for conversion; at the same time they accepted the loan of six of the American versions, the first of which to be commissioned was HMS Archer (ex USS Mormacland) in November 1941. She was followed by three others during the next six months, the Avenger, Biter and Dasher.

Although the intention had been for these ships to take part in convoy escort duties, where they were desperately needed to fill the mid-Atlantic gap which shore-based aircraft could not cover, the general shortage of carriers available and the need for sea-borne fighter cover foreseen as a vital requirement for the huge, impending Allied landings in North Africa, led the British to allocate them for this purpose. This entailed further modifications, and together with numerous early 'teething troubles', this delayed their entry into effective service until late in 1942.

The Avenger, however, was first to demonstrate her value when, in August 1942, she was included in the escort of Convoy PQ18 to North Russia. The previous convoy on this route, PQ17, had met with disaster to which German torpedo planes and bombers stationed in northern Norway had largely contributed. The Avenger was therefore primarily to provide fighter defence, for which she embarked 12 operational Sea Hurricanes and six spares. Only three Swordfish for anti-submarine operations were carried; but they proved of value out of all proportion to their small numbers, locating and driving off threatening U-boats on 16 occasions and sharing in the destruction of three of them.

In the fighter defence rôle, the carrier started badly, her Hurricanes being dispersed chasing shadowing aircraft when a bombing attack by six Junker 88's, followed quickly by a massed torpedo attack by more than

50 Heinkel 111's and Junker 88's, developed. Eight ships of the convoy were lost. Though a further small attack was met by the Hurricanes, six of the enemy being shot down and the convoy escaping unharmed, the Avenger's captain, as he ruefully confessed in his report, realised that his operation of the ship and her fighters had been wrong. The next day he was ready for the attacks when they came.

To meet the first – 22 torpedo planes streaking in low – 9 Hurricanes were flown off and swooped into action. Eleven of the enemy were seen to crash; others jettisoned their torpedoes and fled; the convoy escaped unscathed. A bombing attack which followed was no more successful. Then came a further interlude of intense sound and fury as yet another massed torpedo attack by 25 Heinkels was intercepted, the Hurricanes clinging doggedly to their tails as they flew into the almost solid barrage laid down by the escorts and the merchantmen themselves. Three of the fighters fell victims to it, but the pilots were quickly rescued by escorts. Only one torpedo found a billet, but it was in a ship loaded with ammunition. In the resultant explosion the ship disintegrated, the next ship astern was damaged and a Heinkel was destroyed by the blast.

Sporadic bombing which continued for another hour achieved nothing. When the day ended the attacking planes had clearly taken a bad beating; 24 had been seen to crash, out of which the Hurricanes claimed five certain kills and three probables, while another 14 had departed damaged on the long flight back to base. The total German losses, in fact, out of 337 aircraft sent against the convoy, of which 102 were torpedo planes, amounted to 33 torpedo planes, six Junker 88 bombers and two long-range reconnaissance aircraft.

The result was to be seen the following day when, although up to 70 German bombers arrived above the overcast under which the convoy was steaming, they risked only momentary dives out of the clouds to drop their bombs at random before climbing hurriedly to safety again. Nor were the Germans any bolder or more successful after the Avenger left with the remainder of the ocean escort to join the homeward-bound convoy; PQ18 completed its journey to Russia with no further losses. The homeward convoy was left severely alone by the Luftwaffe.

The *Avenger's* performance with PQ18 had been a splendid demonstration of the value of the escort carrier both for anti-submarine and fighter defence purposes. Had she and her sisters been now allocated to escort duty with the transatlantic convoys, the heavy losses on that route during the coming winter and the early

where British escort carriers played a vital rôle during the landings at Salerno, and in the Pacific where American CVE's comprised the air element of Assault Forces in every island assault. But it was in the wastes of mid-Atlantic that they were to make their greatest impact in the European theatre.

There the long drawn Battle of the Atlantic had reached its critical stage, with the U-boats in large wolf-packs concentrating against the convoys in the 'Black Gap', where air escort could only be intermittently

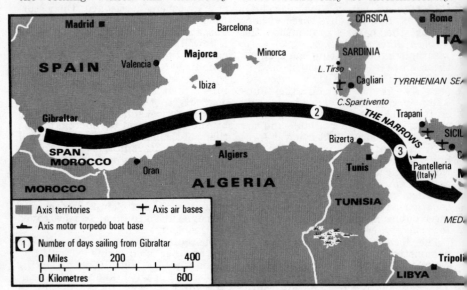

months of 1943 might have been avoided and the crisis of the Battle of the Atlantic overcome so much sooner.

Operation 'Torch', the Anglo-American landings in North Africa in November 1942 intervened, however. The *Dasher*, *Avenger* and *Biter* were all required to provide fighter cover until the Allied Air Forces had been able to establish themselves on airfields ashore. The *Archer*, finally overcoming her early defects, also arrived on the scene as escort for an American troop convoy, as did the first four American converted tankers, *Sangamon*, *Chenango*, *Suwannee* and *Santee*.

These utility carriers were to prove invaluable in such amphibious operations, both in the Mediterranean,

provided by the meagre force of Very Long Range Liberator aircraft allocated – the remainder of those supplied to Britain being absorbed by the strategic bombing campaign against Germany. Elsewhere the air and surface escorts' combined efforts were a match for the wolf packs; but in the 'Black Gap' the surface escorts, bereft of air support, were often swamped by superior numbers and disastrous losses suffered in their convoys.

By March 1943 sinkings were so numerous that the whole convoy system was for a while called in question. The number of VLR aircraft was increased from 17 to rise to a total of 30 by the end of March. But more important, that month saw the first escort carrier begin operations with the convoys. This was the USS *Bogue*. She achieved nothing spectacular at that time; convoy escort was essentially an unspectacular affair; but so long as her Avenger aircraft were in operation, the U-boats, constantly forced to submerge, were prevented from achieving attacking positions and the convoys steamed safely through the submarine patrol lines waiting for them.

In April, the first British support group centred on the escort carrier *Biter* came into operation with nine

Swordfish and three Martlets embarked. Sent to support a westbound convoy threatened by a concentration of U-boats, her aircraft shared in the destruction of a submarine, one of two sunk during the operation; but, more important, the convoy passed scatheless through the U-boat concentration. Even more impressive was the week of skirmishing with the U-boat packs trying to concentrate on the two homeward-bound convoys the *Biter* next supported. In spite of thick and tempestuous weather in which probably only the sturdy and manageable Swordfish could have operated from a small carrier's heaving deck, on nine occasions submarines were detected and put down, one of them being sunk in

co-operation with the surface escorts called up. Both convoys passed through the U-boat concentration without loss.

In May, both the *Bogue* and the *Archer* were equally successful in fighting convoys safely through. The former achieved the first U-boat kill by an escort carrier's plane on the 22nd when one of her Avengers attacked *U 569*. The next day a Swordfish from *Archer*, armed with rocket projectiles, had a similar success in sinking *U 752*.

All this, with the increase in VLR aircraft, added up to the closing of the 'Black Gap', and with it, victory in the Battle of the Atlantic. For during May no less than 41 U-boats were sunk, 25 of them by the convoy air and surface escorts; the U-boat commanders were unable to press home their attacks; convoy losses became suddenly negligible; on May 22, Admiral Dönitz threw in the sponge, so far as the North Atlantic convoys were concerned, and recalled all his U-boats.

They were now deployed further south to attack convoys on the route from the United States to North Africa where another 'gap' outside range of shore-based aircraft attracted them. They were soon defeated there also, however, and again by escort carriers operating in Hunter-Killer Groups. Aircraft from the USS *Bogue*, *Core*, *Santee*, *Card* and *Block Island* sank no less than 24 U-boats during the last seven months of 1943. During 1944, US escort carrier groups sank 16 U-boats, including one captured intact by the USS *Guadalcanal* and her escorts. In the same period British escort carrier groups accounted for 17 U-boats, the majority in Arctic waters while escorting convoys to Russia.

Before we return to the Pacific theatre to follow the course of the vast operations in which the carrier, massed in powerful Task Groups to form the greatest fleet the world has ever known, dominated the scene, it is worth recording one final carrier operation in European waters. Insignificant in comparison to those in the Pacific, it was nevertheless large by European standards and of interest as an example of the dethronement of the battleship by the ship-borne aircraft.

**Attack on the *Tirpitz*: *Above*:
the aircraft approach, flying low
to evade radar detection;
Right: the Germans try to conceal
the *Tirpitz* under a heavy smoke screen**

The German battleship *Tirpitz*, since
her arrival in Norwegian waters early
in 1942, had posed a constant threat to
the passage of convoys to North Russia
and forced on the British the necessity
to maintain a large Home Fleet
against the possibility of her breaking
out into the Atlantic. Several
attempts to eliminate her by RAF
bomber attacks had failed, but in
September 1943 she had been heavily
damaged in a gallant and skilful
operation by British midget submarines. This had put her out of
action for six months; but by March
1944 it was known that she was
repaired and ready to go to sea for
trials.

By this time, the British Fleet Air
Arm had re-equipped a number of its
squadrons with Grumman Hellcat
and Vought Corsair fighters, as well
as Wildcats Mk V, which had the
necessary range to escort a force of

the new Barracuda torpedo/dive-
bomber aircraft and it was decided to
mount an attack using this combination. From the fleet carriers *Victorious*
and *Furious* two striking forces of 21
Barracudas each were to be launched
with 40 fighter escorts for each strike
from the fleet carriers and the escort
carriers *Emperor*, *Searcher*, *Fencer* and
Pursuer.

Preliminary practices and re-
hearsals were mounted on a bombing
and air firing range located in Loch
Eriboll, a deep inlet on the northern
coast of Scotland, before the carrier
force assembled on the afternoon of 2nd
April 1944 some 220 miles to the north-
westward of Altenfiord, near the North
Cape. There the *Tirpitz* lay behind
torpedo nets and surrounded by a ring
of smoke generators which could
shroud her from view in a matter of
minutes. At dawn the next morning
the flying-off position was reached,
some 120 miles from the target.

In clear blue weather, the first strike
of 21 Barracudas from the *Victorious*
and their fighter escorts from the
Victorious, *Pursuer*, *Emperor* and
Searcher took off and, skimming the
wave tops to avoid detection by enemy
radar, headed away for the target.

The Barracudas were variously armed, some with 1,600-pound armour-piercing bombs, others with 500-pound semi-armour piercing, while a few carried fragmentation bombs, calculated to cause casualties to personnel, or anti-submarine bombs, near misses by which might, it was hoped, cause under-water damage. Of the fighters, the Corsairs were to provide top cover while the Hellcats and Wildcats were to strafe the AA guns on shore and on the *Tirpitz*.

50 miles out from the shore, the force climbed to 8,000 feet and soon afterwards the first alarm bells rang through the *Tirpitz*, which was in the process of weighing anchor and getting clear of her net protections. Already the smoke from the generators was drifting across her; but it was still only partly covering the ship when the Hellcats and Wildcats, skimming the surrounding hilltops, swooped to strafe the AA batteries on the shore and the *Tirpitz* herself where the main flak battery and the flak fire controls were put out of action.

The Barracudas followed, diving from 8,000 feet to complete their attack in the space of one minute,

scoring numerous hits, wounding the *Tirpitz's* captain and spreading confusion through the whole ship. One Barracuda was shot down and the crew killed. The remainder escaped unscathed.

At about the same time the second strike was starting on its way, 19 Barracudas from the two fleet carriers, 39 fighters from the *Victorious, Pursuer, Emperor* and *Searcher*. The smoke screen was fully developed by the time they arrived over the target; but it proved more embarrassing to the *Tirpitz's* flak batteries than to the bombers who had little difficulty in aiming their bombs which again scored several hits. The defending AA batteries, blinded by the smoke, succeeded in shooting down only one bomber and none of the strafing fighters. Hit by 14 bombs, the battleship was severely damaged, and though she was able to put to sea again three months later, she never became fully operational and was relegated to a coastal defence role at Tromso. There she was finally destroyed by 12,000 pound bombs dropped by the RAF.

Grappling in the central blue

With the evacuation of Guadalcanal by the Japanese in February 1943, the Pacific War assumed the shape, on the one hand, of an American island-hopping advance up the chain of the Solomons and on to the Bismarck Archipelago; on the other, of an Allied offensive to eject the Japanese from New Guinea. For neither side were such operations, conducted within close range of land air bases, suitable for the intervention of carriers.

And, indeed, neither side were for a time in any position to use their carriers offensively. The Japanese had lost so many carrier-qualified aviators who could not be quickly replaced that they deployed their remaining carrier air groups on the island air bases where they suffered a steady attrition until November 1943 when the remnants were re-embarked and the fleet carriers returned to Japan to rehabilitate and refit. The American carrier strength, following the Battle of the Santa Cruz Islands, was for a while reduced to the single, partially repaired *Enterprise*. An appeal to their British ally resulted in the despatch of the *Victorious* and,

though by the time she had been re-equipped with American aircraft and modified to handle them, the *Saratoga* had completed repairs, the two carriers operated together out of Nouméa for some months, allowing the *Enterprise* to return home for full repairs to be completed.

Meanwhile both sides were striving to rebuild their carrier strength. In this the Americans, with their vast industrial and ship-building capacity and reserves of suitable man-power for training as naval aviators, held an overwhelming advantage. A large construction programme of fleet carriers of the 27,100 ton *Essex* class had been laid down before the outbreak of war, ships with a speed of 33 knots and, fitted with two centre-line and one ship-side elevators, capable of operating more than 100 aircraft. The name ship of the class was commissioned on the last day of 1942. In addition, early in 1942, five 10,000 ton light cruisers under construction had been taken in hand for conversion to smaller (11,000 ton) but fast (32 knots) carriers which could operate some 35 planes. The first of this class, the

Independence, was completed in January 1943. By the fall of 1943, six of the former and five of the latter class were operational with the Pacific Fleet.

In contrast the Japanese programme for six fleet carriers of the 29,300 ton *Taiho* class, 15 of the 17,150 ton *Unryu* class and the conversion of the *Shinano*, third of the *Yamato*-class battleships to be laid down, did not get under way until the middle of 1942. The design of *Taiho*, the first and, in the event, the only one of her class to be built, incorporated the lessons of Midway in that she had a stoutly armoured flight deck and elevators as well as side armour comparable to that of a battleship. She was also lavishly armed with AA guns, equipped with radar and could operate 63 aircraft. She would not be ready for service until 1944, however.

Of the *Unryu* class, only the name ship and one other, the *Amagi*, were ever to be completed, the former coming into service late in 1944 only to be sunk by a US submarine in December of that year before ever being in action. The *Amagi*, though completed at about the same time,

After Guadalcanal, both sides in the Pacific strove to rebuild their carrier strength. An American 27,100 ton carrier of the Essex class, capable of operating over 100 aircraft

never saw active service. Two light fleet carriers were added at about this time, however, by the conversion of the seaplane tenders *Chitose* and *Chiyoda* which had a speed of 29 knots and could operate 30 aircraft each.

Like the British and Americans, the Japanese were also converting some merchant ships into auxiliary carriers but not in the same large numbers. Three ships of the *Taiyo* class of 20,000 tons had already been completed with a speed of only 21 knots and operating 23 aircraft, but these were used mainly for ferrying aircraft to island bases or for deck-landing training of pilots. Two more, the *Shinyo* of 17,500 tons and the *Kaiyo* of 13,600 tons, would be commissioned at the end of 1943, both too slow to operate with the fleet.

Comparison of aircraft in use by the opposing fleets shows the reversal of the advantage held by the Japanese in

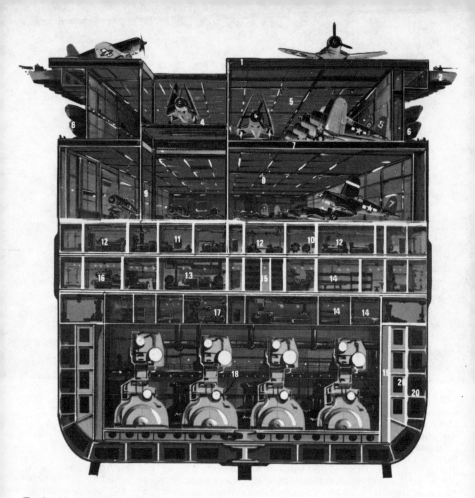

Typical cross section of an aircraft carrier

1 Main flight deck. 2 20 mm A.A. armament.* 3 40 mm A.A. armament.* 4 Aircraft lift.
5 Main aircraft hanger. 6 Some of ship's boats. 7 Heavy armoured deck. 8 Lower
hanger where major servicing and repairs take place. 9 Aircraft lift goes down
to this deck. 10 Engine repair and servicing. 11 Lift machinery. 12 Workshops* 13 Fan
rooms for air conditioning and ventilation.* 14 One of many small crew messes.
15 Engineering (aircraft) stores. One of many.* 16 Lighting plant (aux).* 17 Auxillary
engine room services deck. 18 Turbine room. 19 Fireproof cofferdam.*
20 Aviation fuel tanks. 21 Oil fuel. *There are many of these in the ship.

the early carrier battles. The fighter plane operated by them was still the Zero. Though modified versions had increased its performance, it was outclassed by the Grumman Hellcat which was now the standard American carrier-borne fighter. Similarly the replacement of the Devastator by the the Grumman Avenger and the provision of better torpedoes at last gave the Americans an effective torpedo or bomber strike plane. A less satisfactory change was the replacement of the well-tried Dauntless dive-bomber in many of the carriers by the Curtiss Helldiver.

During 1943, therefore, the American carrier force greatly outstripped that of the Japanese in both size and quality and, in May of that year, it was decided to make use of this superiority to initiate a new strategy to supplement that of MacArthur's methodical advance up the island chains to the Philippines. This was to comprise a drive through the Central Pacific directly at the heart of the Japanese defence system by a series of amphibious assaults on the island bases. The US Fifth Fleet, commanded by Vice Admiral R A Spruance, was formed for the purpose with two amphibious Attack Forces, the Northern, Task Force 52, assembling and training in Hawaii, the Southern, Task Force 53, in the South Pacific. Each of these had its own force of escort carriers and surface warships to give close air support. The fleet carriers were formed into four Task Groups which combined to form Task Force 50. This carrier striking force would be used to soften up the defences of the bases to be captured and neutralise others from which support could be provided. The first objectives were Tarawa and Makin in the Gilbert Islands which were captured between 20th and 23rd November 1943.

The Fifth Fleet next turned its attention to the Marshall Islands at the end of January 1944 when Kwajalein and Majuro Atolls were captured after the carriers and shore-based naval air forces from Tarawa had neutralised the neighbouring islands. The next main objective was the Marianas, the assault on which was scheduled for June 1944. A preliminary was the capture of Eniwetok and while this

was taking place, the great mobility of fast carrier forces was made use of to strike at Truk and the Marianas, 600 miles apart. At the former main naval base, besides 270 aircraft put out of action, two cruisers, four destroyers, 19 transports and five tankers were sunk and the Japanese forced to withdraw the Combined Fleet first to Palau and later to Singapore. At Guam, Saipan and Tinian in the Marianas a large force of bombers, freshly arrived from Japan, was destroyed before it could interfere.

The losses suffered by the Japanese up to this time had been of outposts only. The Marianas, on the other hand, were a part of their main defensive perimeter and a vital staging post in their line of communications with the southern regions. A threat to them would have to be opposed by the full force of the Combined Fleet which was now reorganised under its new C-in-C, Admiral Soemu Toyoda, who exercised his command from his headquarters in Japan[1].

Sea command of what was now renamed the Mobile Fleet was given to Vice Admiral Jisaburo Ozawa who had superseded Nagumo in command of the 3rd Fleet after the Battle of Santa Cruz Islands. It was organised in three groups. The Van Force, under Vice-Admiral Kurita, comprised the three light fleet carriers, *Chitose*, *Chiyoda* and *Zuiho* operating under the shield of the main battle squadron – *Yamato*, *Musashi*, *Haruna* and *Kongo*, four cruisers and a destroyer screen. Force A, under Ozawa himself, with his flag in the carrier *Taiho*, accompanied by the *Shokaku* and *Zuikaku* provided the main air strength with some 200 aircraft. Force B under Rear Admiral Joshima, was grouped round the light carrier *Ryujo* and the larger *Junyo* and *Hiyo*. The total air strength was 430 planes.

When on 15th June 1944 news of American troops landing on Saipan reached the Japanese High Command, this was the fleet that sailed from its advanced base at Tawi Tawi in the

[1] Yamamoto had been shot down and killed when his plane was ambushed over Buin in April 1943. Admiral Koga, his successor, had disappeared with a flying-boat in which he was travelling in March 1944.

Vice Admiral R A Spruance, commanding US Fifth Fl...

Grumman Avengers over the South Pacific. With an effective torpedo at last provided, they formed the chief weapon in the American torpedo strike force

Small but fast American carrier of the Independence class, capable of operating some 35 aircraft. Five were in commission in the Pacific by Autumn 1943

Japanese aircraft-carrier *Unryu*. Although 15 were planned, only two were ever completed

Sulu Archipelago and steered out into the Philippine Sea to give battle. The force it was challenging had by this time grown to seven fleet carriers and eight light fleet carriers, forming Task Force 58, divided into four Task Groups, each with its screen of cruisers and destroyers, operating nearly 900 aircraft commanded by Vice Admiral Marc Mitscher and a further Task Group of seven battleships and four cruisers. Greatly improved radar, radio communications and fighter direction experience and expertise enabled this vast force to be operated and manoeuvred as one body and to defend itself against air attack to a degree never dreamed of during the earlier carrier battles.

The Japanese plan, however, relied upon being able to bring into play a large number of naval aircraft from its wide-spread island air bases to balance the odds against them before any fleet action was joined. Ozawa's sortie was known to Spruance on the 16th from a sighting report from an American submarine patrolling off the San Bernadino Strait. At that time two of Spruance's carrier groups were away attacking the airfields on Iwo Jima and Chichi Jima more than 600 miles north of Saipan; but calculations showed that Ozawa could not be within striking distance until the 19th; the carrier groups could complete the neutralisation of the two islands before rendezvousing 180 miles west of the Marianas at noon on the 18th.

For Spruance had no intention of rushing forward to give battle. He remembered the Japanese propensity for complex strategical plans and for offering a tempting lure. The latter in this case could well be staged to draw him off while a powerful Japanese force circled round to fall upon the assault forces off Saipan, the defence of which was Spruance's primary responsibility. By the afternoon of the 18th his fleet had concentrated three of its carrier groups, 58.1, 58.3 and 58.2, being disposed on a line 15 miles apart in that order from north to south, while 15 miles to the westward – in the direction of the enemy – was Task Group 58.7, the 'Battle Line' of heavy ships to provide a shield of massed gunfire, with the fourth carrier group, 58.4, twelve miles north of it to give fighter protection.[1]

In the meantime Ozawa had spent the daylight hours of the 17th refuelling his ships from his force of replenishment tankers before resuming his eastward course. His three groups were disposed in a rough triangle of which the apex, nearest to the enemy,

[1] For details of the various Task Groups, see Appendix I

was Kurita's Van Force, where it was expected to attract the enemy's attacks, diverting them away from the large carriers and receiving them with the massive gunfire of the battle-ships and cruisers. A hundred miles to the rear were the other two groups, 15 miles apart.

Although a part of Ozawa's fleet was sighted and reported by the US submarine *Cavalla* on the evening of the 17th, the message did not reach Spruance until early on the following morning by which time the information was too 'stale' to be acted upon. The superiority of Japanese naval air reconnaissance was now demonstrated. While Spruance received no further information of the Japanese fleet throughout the 18th from the shore-based planes seeking it, float planes from Ozawa's Van Group, which had been catapulted, had by the early afternoon, located three of the groups of Task Force 58 at a distance of 400 miles.

This was outside the range of American carrier planes but inside that of the Japanese and, with the object of keeping it so, Ozawa steered south-westerly during that night and prepared to strike the next morning. Meanwhile Spruance, too, anxious to keep within supporting distance of his assault groups off Saipan, had turned away eastwards at dusk. When, at 22.00, Pearl Harbor signalled to say that direction-finding stations placed the enemy fleet 350 miles W S W of him, he kept to his decision in spite of a suggestion from the Commander Task Force 58 – Vice Admiral Marc Mitscher – that course should be reversed so as to be in a position to strike at dawn. At about the same time a naval flying boat located Ozawa 600 miles west of Saipan; but it was not until 09.00 the following morning that this vital message reached Spruance, too late to be of real use. His own search by carrier planes launched at dawn failed to make contact.

In contrast, seaplanes and carrier scout planes from Ozawa's Van Force had regained contact and, although many were intercepted far out by the combat air patrol from TG58.4 and shot down, Ozawa was in possession of the information he needed to launch his first striking force composed of 45 Zero fighter-bombers, eight torpedo planes and 16 Zero fighter escorts from the carriers of the Van Force at 08.30, followed half an hour later by 53 Val dive-bombers, 27 torpedo Kates and an escort of 48 Zero's from the big fleet carriers of Force 'A'. At 09.30 yet another strike, 47 aircraft strong was on its way from Force 'B'.

While the carrier groups were thus busily engaged, manoeuvring at high speed, turning into wind to launch

131

and recover planes, an episode had taken place which seemed at the time of minor importance. Ozawa's fleet had reached a patrol line of four American submarines cunningly deployed to intercept him. Through the periscope of one of them, the *Albacore,* Commander Blanchard saw the sight of all sights to gladden a submariner's heart, Ozawa's fine new flagship, the *Taiho,* on a steady course into wind, flying off aircraft. A last-minute breakdown of the submarine's torpedo data computer nearly robbed Blanchard of his triumph; but one of

Nearly 400 miles to the eastward, Task Force 58 had been similarly busily engaged. Since dawn, Hellcats of the combat air patrols had been aloft in the cloudless blue Pacific sky. Others had been in action over Guam where, in accordance with the Japanese plan, aircraft had been arriving from the other island bases to join in the attack on the American fleet. They were far fewer than had been visualised in the plan and the opposition they met much greater – a result of Spruance's cautious refusal to advance too far from the islands.

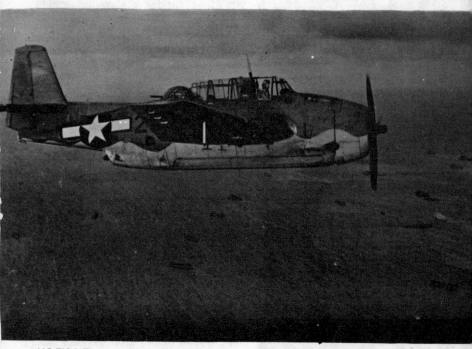

US Fifth Fleet at the Marshall Islands, January 1944

his torpedoes struck home.

Well armoured as she was, the *Taiho* was far from lethally damaged, it seemed, or even crippled. But behind the protective armour, the shock of explosion had, all unknown, caused a crack in a tank containing aviation gasoline. A chain of events had been started which was to come to a head six hours later. Meanwhile the carrier remained in action and continued to operate her aircraft.

By 10.00 the airfields on Guam had been temporarily neutralised and Mitscher was able to recall his fighters.

It was just in time: for at that moment the first swarm of Japanese strike planes was detected on the radar of the Battle Line at a range of 150 miles. The vast array of carriers turned into the wind. From their decks a stream of aircraft took off and climbed away. Any bombers or torpedo planes which had been ranged on deck were sent away to orbit to the eastward to keep decks clear for fighters; then the Hellcats roared off, the first of a series to be launched, to go into action, land on again and be refuelled and re-armed and launched again in rotation throughout the day, a total of some 300 being thus engaged, intercepting either incoming carrier strikes or enemy aircraft making for Guam.

What followed was to be called by the exulting American airmen 'The Great Marianas Turkey Shoot'. For Spruance's strategy, criticised as it was to be by many as too cautious, enabled him to oppose an almost impenetrable defence to the Japanese

strikes. Long before they reached their objectives, Hellcats in over-whelming numbers swarmed on to them, some engaging the escorting Zeros over which they held a decisive advantage in performance, others sending the luckless Kates and Vals plunging, flaming down to stain the blue waters with the black debris of their destruction. Barely a handful of strike planes managed to break through to face the massed gunfire of the battleships, cruisers and des-troyers. They succeeded only in inflicting minor damage on the

carriers *Wasp* and *Bunker Hill*. Some thirty survivors out of the 200 aircraft of the first two strikes were all that straggled back to their carriers to tell an imaginative tale of American carriers ablaze and sinking.

The third strike, of forty-seven air-craft from Force 'B', strayed too far to the north; half of them failed to find any target and returned to base; the remainder succeeded in locating the northern American carrier group and bore down to the attack. Hellcats shot down seven of them; others broke through only to drop their bombs hastily and ineffectively before escaping.

Before the magnitude of this failure became known to Ozawa his carrier group suffered catastrophe as, at 1220, the *Shokaku* staggered under the shock of the explosion of three tor-pedoes. They came from the sub-marine *Cavalla* which, after the earlier location of the Japanese fleet, had chased doggedly through the night and been rewarded by finding herself in an ideal attacking position when Force 'A' turned into wind to recover aircraft. With smoke and flames pouring from petrol fires, the *Shokaku* limped out of action. For the next three hours desperate efforts to master the fires were repeatedly nullified as petrol fumes spreading through the ship exploded. The end came for this veteran of every carrier battle since Pearl Harbor except Midway, as one final explosion tore her open and sent her to the bottom.

At almost the same time disaster overtook Ozawa's flagship. From the ruptured gasoline tank, fumes had been gathering. To clear them, the order was given to turn on the venti-lation system throughout the ship. It was a fatal move, spreading the explosive gases until, inevitably, a spark ignited them, causing a heavy explosion, setting the ship ablaze and tearing open her hull. The *Taiho* was clearly doomed. Ozawa and his staff were transferred to the cruiser *Haguro* and the order to abandon ship was given. Only 500 of her crew of 2,150 had been taken off, when a further heavy explosion occurred and the carrier capsized and sank.

In spite of these daunting cata-strophes, the Japanese, encouraged by

the claims of returning pilots, continued doggedly to attack. From the last remaining fleet carrier, *Zuikaku*, and from the three light carriers of Force 'B', another strike of eighty-seven planes was despatched. Misdirected, they steered too far south. They were also instructed to make for Guam after completing their attacks, to refuel and re-arm, the true state of affairs over and on the island airfields not having been frankly reported to Ozawa. Less than half of them located the southern carrier group, made an ineffective attack and were mostly shot down. The remainder, forty-nine strong, carried on for Guam and its cratered runways. Set upon by twenty-seven Hellcats, thirty of them plummeted, blazing into the sea or on to the airfield as they tried to land.

By 1600 the air over the American fleet had been swept clear of enemy aircraft. Fighting continued over Guam and Rota, for a few hours more as the Japanese tried to feed reinforcements in, only to have them shot down in the act of landing or crash on the bombed runways. Although

Ozawa, his signal facilities limited in his makeshift flagship, did not yet know the details, out of 373 aircraft which had been launched from his carriers, only 130 had returned. 'Operational' losses, running at a high rate amongst his inexperienced pilots, accounted for more carrier aircraft so that when night fell on the 19th only 102 remained on board out of the 430 with which he had set out. Another fifty shore-based aircraft had also been destroyed during the day.

Spruance's defensive tactics had been to some extent forced on him by his lack of accurate knowledge of the enemy's whereabouts. But there can be little doubt they were correct, leading, as they did, to such an annihilation of Japanese trained carrier air crews, losses which could not be replaced in time to intervene in the war. The cost to the Americans had been only twenty-three aircraft shot down, with six more operational losses. Not a ship had been seriously damaged.

With the enemy's air power so crushed, Spruance was at last able to go over to the offensive. Leaving

one of his carrier task groups (TG58.4) to cover the amphibious force off Saipan, he headed westwards at his best speed through the night with the remainder, hoping that by the dawn he would have information of the enemy's position that would enable him to launch a strike. He was to be disappointed. His shore-based distant reconnaissance failed to locate and shadow the enemy and meanwhile Ozawa, too, had turned away north-westward to make rendezvous with his replenishment tankers. He was thus out of range of the search planes launched from T.F.58 at dawn.

While Spruance continued to press on westwards during the forenoon and afternoon of the 20th, Ozawa, still under the impression that his aviators had inflicted huge losses on the Americans on the previous day, had rejected the advice of Kurita, his less credulous second-in-command, to cut his losses and head for Japan; instead he prepared to refuel his force prior to resuming the attack. Only about 100 planes remained operational on board his carriers, but he believed that many were safely down on Guam and available to take part.

The decision was a fatal one, the delay allowing a search plane from the *Enterprise* to come up at last with him at about 1600. It was late in the day; the enemy was only just within striking range of the American planes; but though it meant recovering his pilots, untrained for night flying, after dark, Marc Mitscher appealed to be allowed to launch them. Spruance concurred, and within half an hour of the enemy report, seventy-seven dive-bombers and fifty-four torpedo planes with an escort of eighty-five fighters were taking off and heading into the setting sun.

It was already dusk when they sighted their target and, sweeping aside the thin screen of Zeros which was all that could be mustered, swooped down to the attack. For the loss of fourteen aircraft, they torpedoed and sank the carrier *Hiyo*; the *Zuikaku* was hit by several bombs, starting a conflagration that nearly proved fatal; the *Chiyoda* was also set on fire and had her flight deck mangled. A battleship and a cruiser were damaged by bombs. Out of the 190

aircraft with which Ozawa had started the day, only thirty-five survived. The Japanese Admiral at last accepted his total defeat and, as he fled through the night towards Okinawa he signalled his resignation, which was not accepted.

Meanwhile the American planes were streaming back along the 300 mile route to their carriers into the growing darkness with, for many of the pilots, a first night deck landing ahead of them. Night fell over Mitscher's carriers. Disregarding any risks from enemy bombers or submarines he ordered every form of illumination – star shell, searchlights, navigation lights, flight-deck floodlights. In spite of all this, no less than eighty planes crashed on deck or splashed in the sea as their fuel ran out. Few of their crews were lost, however. Wide-spread rescue operations were mounted during the night and following day; when they were over, only sixteen pilots and thirty-three aircrew were missing from the whole operation.

The greatest carrier battle of all time and one of the most decisive battles of the war was over. That a large part of the Japanese Fleet had

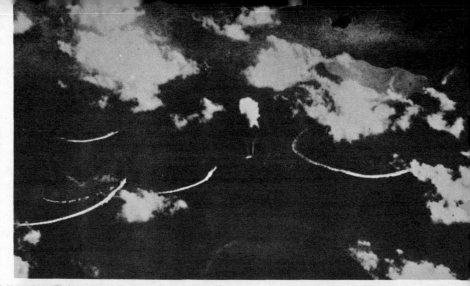

'The Great Marianas Turkey Shoot' as the American pilots named
the battle, was an affair of great confusion at sea-level

escaped destruction was to arouse criticism of Spruance's cautious strategy, particularly from the US naval aviators who, probably rightly, considered that a Halsey would have taken a bolder line. But whether such action would have achieved a greater success is doubtful. If the two sides had exchanged simultaneous blows as in earlier carrier battles, more Japanese ships would perhaps have been sunk; but casualties on the American side might also have been heavy.

As it was, Spruance had virtually wiped out Japanese naval air power at a cost almost miraculously small for a victory of such magnitude. Though the *Zuikaku, Junyo, Chitose, Chiyoda, Zuiho* and *Ryujo* escaped, the Japanese were never to be able to train replacement aircrews for them. When the final battle came, the survivors would be 'toothless tigers' offered up in the traditional Japanese strategy, as sacrificial decoys.

Sovereign of the seas

So tremendous were the losses of Japanese naval aircraft during the Battle of the Philippine Sea and the carrier operations in support of the capture of the Marianas, so shattering to Japanese morale was the breach in their defences represented by the loss of Saipan (it led to the resignation of General Tojo's Cabinet), that the US Chiefs of Staff came to the conclusion that a short cut to ending the war with Japan was open.

Instead of the slow and costly island-hopping strategy of General MacArthur, it was proposed that the next objective after the Marianas should be Formosa, by-passing the whole island complex further south, including the Philippines. This, however, came up against the inflexible determination of General MacArthur to reconquer the Philippines and rescue its people as early as possible and to honour his promise made when he was forced to abandon them – 'I will return'.

A compromise was eventually reached in which it was planned for MacArthur, reinforced by the Central Pacific Assault Forces and by the air strength of the Pacific Fleet's carriers, to by-pass the stepping stones on the island route to the Philippines and make one bold leap from New Guinea across 1,500 miles of sea to the Philippine island of Leyte. The date for the landing in the Gulf of Leyte was fixed for 20th October 1944.

The fleet which had won the Battle of the Philippine Sea had meanwhile been re-designated the 3rd Fleet while Halsey relieved Spruance under a system of alternating command in which one commander and his staff would be planning the succeeding operation from a headquarters at Pearl Harbor while the other commanded at sea. Task Force 58 had thus become TF 38 though the ships were the same and Marc Mitscher remained in command of it. Starting on 10th October, TF 38 pounded Japanese air bases in Okinawa, Formosa and northern Luzon from which interference with the Leyte operation could be mounted.

In reply came large numbers of 'Betty' twin-engined torpedo planes to make twilight and night attacks. They suffered heavily, losing forty of their number, and succeeded only in

Admiral Halsey and his staff on board the *Enterprise*

torpedoing and damaging two cruisers. The surviving pilots made fantastic claims of large numbers of carriers, battleships and cruisers sunk and others damaged which induced Toyoda to believe a heavy defeat had been inflicted. From Japan the partially trained carrier groups were despatched to Formosa where the commanding admiral, Fukudome, was to use them to complete the annihilation.

Instead, it was they themselves, meeting the massed Hellcats of TF 38 who suffered annihilation. By 16th October, they had been almost totally destroyed and the air strength in Formosa and the Philippines had been reduced to less than 200 planes. The Third Fleet, besides the two damaged cruisers, had suffered only minor damage to three carriers and the loss of ninety planes with sixty-four pilots and aircrew. The majority of Japanese pilots remaining were so untrained and inexperienced that to ensure bomb hits on enemy ships they were invited to volunteer to immolate

themselves in suicide dives. Under the romantic name of *Kamikaze* – the Divine Wind which Japanese history recorded as saving the country from defeat by the Koreans – they now prepared to put such tactics into operation.

The advance units of MacArthur's huge invasion armada arrived in the Gulf of Leyte on 17th October. Supporting the amphibious forces was a Fire Support and Bombardment Group of old battleships, cruisers and destroyers, and three carrier groups, each of six escort carriers, operating to the eastward of the Gulf of Leyte.[1] Once again a challenge had been thrown down that the Japanese Fleet could not ignore, even though, in the face of American air supremacy, to offer battle could only mean defeat. An operational plan 'SHO-1' had been prepared and on the 18th the executive order to carry it out was signalled. From Singapore was to advance Kurita's 1st Striking Force containing all the surviving battleships and all but three of the heavy cruisers. After fuelling at Brunei in North Borneo, it was to divide in two. Force

139

Left: Fighting off the men bent on suicide and glory. US crewmen load their 40 mm guns in a frenzied effort to bring down the aircraft before it hits their ship. *Right:* Kamikaze's near miss: the *USS Sangamon* survives a suicide attack

'A' under Kurita himself, with his flag in the cruiser *Atago*, and the battleships *Yamato, Musashi, Nagato, Kongo* and *Haruna*, ten cruisers and a screen of light cruisers and destroyers, was to proceed by the Palawan Passage, the Mindoro Strait, the Sibuyan Sea, and the San Bernadino Strait, rounding Samar to approach Leyte from the north, arriving at dawn 25th October. Force 'C' under Vice Admiral Shoji Nishimura, comprising the remaining two battleships, *Yamashiro* and *Fuso*, a cruiser and destroyers, was to make its way through the Mindanao Sea and the Surigao Strait to fall on the invasion force in the Leyte Gulf also at dawn on 25th. It would be supported by a squadron of two cruisers and four destroyers which were to come from Japan under Rear Admiral Kiyohide Shima.

Powerful as these Striking Forces were, and capable of engaging Vice Admiral T C Kinkaid's Seventh Fleet grouped round its squadron of six old battleships, which comprised the naval element of MacArthur's invasion force, they could not hope to survive the massed attacks to be expected from the carriers of TF 38. A scheme was therefore devised, in the classic Japanese mould, whereby the carriers *Zuikaku, Zuiho, Chitose* and *Chiyoda* and the battleships *Ise* and *Hyuga*, which had had their after gun turrets replaced by a small flight deck, would sally forth from the Inland Sea under Ozawa and, approaching from the north, pose an apparent threat to lure TF 38 away for the crucial period.

The carriers had been waiting for the new air groups which were to replace those lost in the Battle of the Philippine Sea. These replacements, still half-trained, had been thrown into the battle off Formosa and massacred. Less than a hundred remained to embark in the four carriers and they were untrained in decklanding; once off they could only make for a shore airfield on completion of their mission. The enemy would not know this, however, and the carriers, it was hoped, would form an irresistible bait for him. The ruse was to be successful beyond Ozawa's wildest hopes and was to come near to providing a last taste of glory for the Imperial Navy before going down to final destruction.

The SHO plan began calamitously for the Japanese. Kurita's Force A was still threading the shoals of the Palawan Passage on the 23rd when, in quick succession, his flagship *Atago* and the cruisers *Takao* and *Maya* were

group discovered Kurita's imposing force skirting the southern end of Mindoro to enter the Sibuyan Sea. Halsey at once ordered his carrier groups to launch striking forces. Task Force 38.3[1] however, was unable to comply. It was too busy beating off a series of massive raids of bombers and torpedo-planes from Luzon air-fields and some – though this was not realised at the time – from Ozawa's carriers, the presence of which, far to the north was not yet known to Halsey.

The attacks were heavy, but, de-

all torpedoed by US submarines *Dace* and *Darter*, only the *Takao* surviving to limp away, heavily damaged, to Singapore. Kurita rehoisted his flag in the *Yamato*; Force 'A' pressed on.

In the Philippine Sea, beyond the San Bernadino Strait, Halsey, having sent TG 38.1 away to replenish at the advanced fleet base of Ulithi in the Carolines, launched search groups from the remainder. One of these located Nishimura's Force C. The news was passed to Kinkaid who took steps to bar the passage through the Surigao Strait. The other search

The Leyte Island landing. A carrier-based Avenger provides air coverage for the landing craft below

livered by half-trained air crews, unskilful. They were uniformly un-successful except for a single dive-bomber, arriving during a lull when the carriers were recovering and refuelling their fighters. Making use of the rain squalls sweeping across the sea, it remained undetected until it

[1] See Appendix II for composition of the units of the 3rd and 7th Fleets.

142

dived out of a low cloud to drop a bomb squarely on the flight deck of the light carrier *Princeton*. In spite of prolonged and heroic efforts to save the ship, which was set furiously ablaze, and during which her bomb store exploded, inflicting more than 630 casualties on board the cruiser *Birmingham* coming alongside to assist, the carrier was finally abandoned and scuttled.

Meanwhile the first of Halsey's striking forces had been launched from the *Intrepid* and *Cabot* of TG 38.2 – twelve dive-bombers, twelve torpedo planes and twenty-one fighters at 0910. For the rest of the day further strikes from the three carrier groups followed one another to make for Kurita's force. The clear blue sky offered them no cover against the storm of gunfire put up by the countless guns and machine guns, including 18.1in shells from the *Yamato* and *Musashi*. They proved more spectacular than effective, however, and no more than eighteen American planes were to be lost during the day. The battleships *Yamato*, *Musashi* and *Nagato* were all hit by bombs but their armoured bulk was little affected. Then at noon the Avengers of two strikes concentrated a co-ordinated attack on the *Musashi*, hitting her with eight torpedoes. Although she dropped astern, crippled, and turned back to make for base, the stoutly built leviathan might yet have survived but for a further concentration of planes from the *Intrepid*, *Cabot*, *Franklin*, *Essex* and *Enterprise* that afternoon which put ten more torpedoes into her. She lingered another four hours before finally rolling over and going to the bottom of the Sibuyan Sea.

The absence of any of the shore-based fighter cover he had expected had meanwhile caused Kurita to reverse course until darkness fell. But by 1910 he was once more steering at twenty knots for the San Bernadino Strait. At this time, too, Nishimura's Force 'C' was approaching the Surigao Strait at the northern end of which Kinkaid's Fire support and Bombardment Group was being deployed under Rear Admiral J B Oldendorf in opposition. Halsey's carriers were gathering in their planes in the last of the daylight while he himself was pondering his next move.

News of Ozawa's carrier force to the northward had at last reached Halsey during the afternoon, the heart of Japanese sea power as they still seemed and which many American naval aviators, including Marc Mitscher, his Task Force Commander, considered had been weakly allowed to escape from the Battle of the Philippine Sea. They constituted a potent lure, as the Japanese had calculated. Halsey's airmen had brought back glowing tales of the destruction wrought on Kurita's Force – 'at least four and probably five battleships torpedoed and bombed, one probably sunk; a minimum of three heavy cruisers torpedoed and others bombed . . .' It could surely no longer be considered a force to be seriously reckoned with! The 7th Fleet could take care of it. At 2000 Halsey gave the order for the three carrier groups with him to steer north to attack Ozawa at dawn. The fourth group was recalled from Ulithi to rejoin at its best speed. To Kinkaid he signalled 'Am proceeding north with three groups to attack the enemy carrier force'.

Unfortunately Kinkaid had earlier intercepted a signal of Halsey's organising the battleships and cruisers attached to the carrier group into a separate Task Force 34. This purely preparative instruction, to be executed if and when required, was misconstrued by the 7th Fleet Commander as a firm order. He now assumed, therefore, that Halsey was departing with his carriers only, leaving the battleships of TF 34 to guard the exit from the San Bernadino Strait. So when during the night Nishimura and Shima were met and annihilated in the Surigao Strait by Rear Admiral Oldendorf's force, the situation seemed well in hand.

In the three groups of escort carriers to the eastward of Leyte Gulf, dawn on 25th October found preparations going on for another day of air support to the troops fighting ashore. The groups were widely spread with Group 1, southernmost of the three, off Mindanao, Group 2 off the entrance to Leyte Gulf, while off Samar was Group 3, the escort carriers *Fanshaw*

Bay, flagship of Rear Admiral Clifton Sprague, *St. Lo, White Plains, Kalinin Bay, Kitkun Bay* and *Gambier Bay* with their screen of three destroyers and three destroyer escorts. Avengers armed with general purpose bombs for ground air support or with depth-charges for anti-submarine patrol had been flown off at first light.

The early morning calm was dramatically shattered in Group 3 when, soon after battleship mast-heads had been sighted on the northern horizon, the startling report from an Avenger on A/S patrol was heard announcing four Japanese battleships, eight cruisers and numerous destroyers only twenty miles away.

In spite of all the rough handling he had suffered at the hands of Halsey's carrier planes on the previous day, Kurita had achieved complete surprise. To the fire of his guns were presented six defenceless ships with little more than half his own speed. At 0659 the first salvoes thundered out. A long, calm and clear day lay ahead in which to wreck destruction not only on the little carriers but on the vast array of the invasion fleet in Leyte Gulf. To all appearances catastrophe had fallen on the US 7th Fleet.

Appealed to by Sprague for assistance, Kinkaid called for Halsey's battleships to intervene, not realising they were with the carriers far away to the north. Halsey, in turn, ordered his fourth Task Group of carriers (38.1) to go to Sprague's assistance, but this group, hurrying to rejoin Halsey after being recalled from replenishing, was still hundreds of miles to the eastward and could not intervene before 1300. Kinkaid's own battle force was three hours steaming away, mopping up after the night's battle in the Surigao Strait and was short of ammunition. Sprague was on his own.

What followed seemed in the aftermath to be nothing short of a miracle. Sprague's only defensive weapons were his Avengers and the guns and torpedoes of his small escort force. Fleeing at his best speed and flying off every aircraft available, covering himself as best he could with smoke-screens, he was to recall later that 'At this point it did not appear that

any of our ships could survive another five minutes.' He ordered his three destroyers into the attack. With superb gallantry they complied, racing in to launch torpedoes, one of which hit the cruiser *Kumano*, knocking her out of the fight; the others forced Kurita's battleships to turn away and give Sprague a vital breathing space. The three destroyer-escorts, lightly armed ships with only three torpedoes each, joined in. All torpedoes expended, the six little ships banged away with their 5in. guns at their powerful opponents and when a

Japanese destroyer squadron led by a light cruiser advanced to the attack, they drove them off.

Such odds could not be faced indefinitely. The destroyers *Hoel* and *Johnston* and the destroyer-escort *Samuel B. Roberts* were sunk: the remainder retired damaged. But they had given time for the aircraft of Sprague's group and from the neighbouring Group 2 to come into action. Bombs and torpedoes from them sank the cruisers *Chikuma* and *Chokai*, while bomb-hits distracted the gunnery of Kurita's other ships and fatally damaged the cruiser *Suzuya*.

Nevertheless one of Sprague's carriers, the *Gambier Bay*, had been hammered to a wreck by enemy gunfire and about 0900 she sank. Three others had been hit and by 0915 the Japanese cruisers had closed to within 10,000 yards and were in position for the kill. Then, under the astonished eyes of the Americans, they suddenly turned away, recalled to rejoin Kurita who, as a result of the gallant attacks of the destroyers was still astern on the horizon.

This incredible development came what next to do. For the next three hours he hesitated, gathering in his scattered ships, and pondering whether to make a bold thrust into Leyte Gulf. At 1236 he finally threw in the sponge, turning away towards the San Bernadino Strait. Half an hour later the first strike of fifty-two bombers from the carriers *Hancock*, *Hornet* and *Wasp* of TG 38.1 arrived to join the harrying of Kurita's ships by the planes of the escort carriers, which had never ceased. Though he suffered only bomb hits on the battleship *Nagato* and the cruiser *Tone* at

USS Wasp, launched in August 1943, was the seventh ship to bear the name. Its predecessor was sunk at Guadalcanal

about as a result of Kurita's belief that the 'flat-tops' he could see in distant silhouette were, in fact, fleet carriers of Halsey's 3rd Fleet. The repeated and daring attacks of the planes from the escort carriers did nothing to disillusion him. His painful experience of the previous day had impressed him with the necessity to act with caution and he had decided to concentrate his force and consider

this time, it was enough to confirm him in his decision to retire. By nightfall he was entering the San Bernadino Strait.

As though the ordeal and the miraculous escape of the escort carriers had not been sufficient drama for the day, Kurita's abandonment of the chase had been the signal for a new and no less deadly menace to assail them. This was the first sortie of Kamikaze planes which selected the southernmost of the three carrier groups as first targets for their suicidal dives. The *Santee* was the first to suffer as a Kamikaze crashed on to her deck. Her crew were still putting out the fires and making action repairs when a torpedo from a Japanese submarine also hit her; but in spite of this she survived – a remarkable credit to her designer and builders – as was the *Suwannee*, which also took a Kamikaze on her flight deck.

When the Kamikaze next turned their attention to Clifton Sprague's northern group, the *Kitkun Bay* was fortunate when one which crashed her flight deck bounced off into the sea before its bomb exploded. Two others were shot down into the sea by the guns of the *Fanshaw Bay* and *White Plains*. But the *St. Lo* had no such luck. The Kamikaze which hit her broke through the flight deck into the hangar where bombs and torpedoes were detonated, tearing the ship apart to sink thirty minutes later. One more attack in which the *Kalinin Bay* survived two Kamikaze hits brought the day's events to a close for the harassed carriers of the 7th Fleet.

Meanwhile, far to the north, Task Force 38 had accepted the so tempting bait offered by Ozawa. Radar-equipped Avengers from the *Independence* had gained contact during the previous night and, with daylight, there began a day-long massacre of the Japanese ships which were able to put up only a negligible fighter defence.

The carrier *Chitose* was the first to be destroyed by a strike force which also torpedoed Ozawa's flagship *Zuikaku*, reducing her speed to eighteen knots, crippled the light-cruiser *Tama* with another torpedo and damaged the *Zuiho* with a bomb. The carrier *Chiyoda* bore the brunt of the next strike, being left immobilised and blazing to be finally disposed of that evening by Halsey's cruisers.

While this had been going on, the situation of the 7th Fleet escort carriers had been spelt out for Halsey in a series of increasingly desperate signals. With the final annihilation of the Japanese carrier fleet in view, however, he resisted all appeals until nearly mid-day; then, at last, he gave in, ordering Task Group 38.2 and four of his battleships to turn back to the rescue. They were to be too late, however, arriving off the San Bernadino Strait three hours after Kurita had escaped through it.

The remainder of Halsey's Task Force pressed on in pursuit of the disentegrating Japanese carrier force. At 1410, the *Zuikaku*, the last survivor of the Pearl Harbor attack, thrice torpedoed by aircraft from the *Lexington*, rolled over and sank. The *Zuiho*, smothered with bomb hits, lasted a little longer, finally sinking at 1526.

Ozawa, who had earlier shifted his flag to the light-cruiser *Oyodo*, survived to know that he had duly played out his tragic, sacrificial role only to have the shaken and vacillating Kurita reject the golden opportunity presented to him. The carriers of Halsey's Task Groups 38.1 and 38.2 resumed the harrying of Kurita's force during 26th October as he fled through the Mindoro Sea. They succeeded in sinking only the light cruiser *Noshiro*. Liberators of the US Army Air Force took up the attack, but a massed raid by forty-seven of them achieved nothing. With the battleships *Yamato*, *Kongo* and *Nagato* and the survivors of his cruisers, Kurita escaped to Japan. But it was the end of the once splendid Imperial Japanese Navy. Never again could it hope to challenge the invincible strength of the US Pacific Fleet.

The ultimate defeat of Japan had been apparent even to fanatical warlords of General Tojo's Government from the time that the Marianas had fallen to the Americans following the Battle of the Philippine Sea. Tojo's Cabinet had resigned to be replaced by one under General Koiso who would have welcomed peace but dared not propose what would have entailed unconditional surrender of Japanese armies in the conquered territories, as yet undefeated. The Battle for Leyte had been a despairing suicidal gesture.

The war was to drag on for another ten months during which the Japanese were to be defeated and driven from Burma and from the Philippines and thence, by-passing Formosa, from Okinawa in the Ryukus, from the numerous airfields of which Japan could be brought under continuous, escorted attack. During this final phase, the US Pacific Fleet roamed at will, acting as a vast mobile air base in support of the land and amphibious operations.

Surface threat by the Japanese Fleet could be ignored particularly after the final sortie of the *Yamato* in April 1945 with fuel only for a one-way passage to the combat area in which she met her end at the hands of American carrier planes without ever sighting the opposing fleet. The American battleships and cruisers were confined to the role of AA escort to the carriers and occasional bombardment missions. The Kamikazes, which had expanded hugely from the handful of initial volunteers, were of fighting against dogged resistance before the island was in American hands. In the course of them the *Saratoga* was crashed by one Kamikaze and hit by the bomb from another. Though she suffered 123 men killed and 192 wounded and had forty-two of her planes destroyed, the veteran carrier was able to steam under her own power to the States for repair. The escort carrier *Bismarck Sea*, however, was sunk by a similar attack and lost 218 of her crew.

The assault on Okinawa, destined to be the last of the great amphibious operations of the Pacific War, was also

The end of the Musashi, October 25th 1944. She was sunk by torpedoes from planes of the US Third Fleet

the main threat.

Prior to the assault on Okinawa, scheduled for 1st April 1945, an operation was mounted to capture the rugged little volcanic island of Iwo Jima in the Bonin Islands where the airfields were required as an emergency landing ground for B-29 bombers on bombing missions from the Marianas to Tokyo. It was to prove one of the bloodiest amphibious operations of the war and take nearly a month to be the most hazardous for the supporting naval forces on account of the numerous Japanese air bases on Formosa, on the Sakishima group of islands between Formosa and Okinawa and on Kyushu, all within range of the fleet's operational area, from which more than 2,000 planes employing kamikaze tactics could be brought into action against the expeditionary force and the supporting fleet.

The American Fleet – at this time once again designated the 5th Fleet and under Admiral's Spruance's command – opened the Okinawa operation on 14th March when Task Force 58

147

USS Franklin, one of the great heroines
of the Pacific war. She was attacked
by dive bombers which scored two hits.
Fires started throughout the vessel
and 1,000 men were killed or injured.
Franklin subsequently limped 12,000
miles to New York City. Above: The ship
is covered in smoke and flames; the
Santa Fe comes alongside, bottom:
and takes on survivors. Above right:
Left: with the flight deck gaping wide
above them, the men attend religious
service

under Marc Mitscher sailed from its advanced anchorage at Ulithi to raid the airfields of southern Japan between 18th and 21st March. The Japanese reply to these attacks on their own soil was predictably fierce. The *Wasp*, *Yorktown* and *Franklin* were all hit by Kamikazes, the last-named suffering 724 men killed and 265 wounded and being so badly damaged that she had to be towed away by a cruiser. The *Wasp* also suffered heavy casualties and was forced to return to the States for repair. The *Yorktown* was able to continue in action. The Japanese paid for these successes with 161 aircraft shot down besides large numbers destroyed on the ground.

TF 58 now turned their attention to the airfields of Okinawa itself. On 26th March they were joined by the British Pacific Fleet under Admiral Sir Bernard Rawlings who placed himself under Admiral Spruance's supreme command. Although composed of only four fleet carriers – *Indomitable*, *Victorious*, *Illustrious* and *Indefatigable* – with an escort of battleships, cruisers and destroyers and so equivalent to a single Task Group of TF 58, is was designated Task Force 57. In this first operation alongside its American Allies, it was assigned a separate group of targets – the airfields of Sakishima Gunto – and operated independently.

To prepare this force for a form of warfare so very different from that in the confined, submarine infested waters of the European theatre had taken a great effort, not only in equipping and training it to operate alongside the experienced veterans of the Pacific War, but in providing the necessary vast logistic backing for operating 3,500 miles from its main base at Sydney N.S.W. The latter, indeed, was never fully achieved before the end of the war.

In preparation for the type of operation waiting for them in the Pacific they had mounted strike operations against the well-defended Japanese-held oil refineries in Sumatra. To be ready to operate as a part of the US Pacific Fleet they had scrapped the whole of their signal system and procedure and adopted those of the US Navy.

So far as combat effectiveness was concerned, the British carriers were handicapped by inferior aircraft in those which had not been re-equipped with American types, the Seafire fighter in particular, a naval adaptation of the Spitfire, being less reliable, less suitable for deck-landing and, above all, having a much lower endurance than its American counterparts. The last of these shortcomings prevented the use of the Seafire as escort for long-range strikes and confined it to the task of combat air patrol over the carriers. The ships themselves were also slower and had less endurance than the American.

In addition the design of the British carriers, with their armoured flight decks and hangers and fire safety precautions permitted them to carry far fewer planes. These defensive characteristics were to prove of vital importance, however, the first occasion being on 1st April when the *Indefatigable's* flight deck was hit by a Kamikaze at the base of the island superstructure. Within a few hours she was operating aircraft again and was able to remain with the Task Force.

During the first five days of the Okinawa operation the Japanese air opposition, composed largely of Kamikazes, concentrated mainly on the landing force. A number of transports were hit and casualties were severe. But these were uncoordinated, individual attacks. Being prepared were far more dangerous massed Kamikaze attacks or 'kikusui'. The first of these, and the largest, in which no less than 355 Kamikazes and 341 other planes – fighter escorts or conventional bombers – took part, was launched on 6th April.

The attacks were divided between the amphibious forces and the carrier task force. In the former an LST and two Victory ships loaded with ammunition were sunk; but it was the destroyers on isolated duties, particularly the radar pickets stationed at a distance round Okinawa and round the carrier force that bore the brunt. Three of them were sunk and seventeen more knocked out of action. But none of this huge force of aircraft broke through to the carriers.

Baka. A revolutionary Japanese weapon, normally carried under a 'Betty' bomber and released 22 miles from target at 27,000 feet. *Speed (diving):* 620 miles per hour. *Max range:* 55 miles. Armament 2645 lb warhead

It was in support of this extravagant effort that the *Yamato* was sent out on the 7th. Perhaps expecting Mitscher's carriers to have been neutralised, she was given no fighter cover. For two hours, beginning at 1232, strike after strike from TF 58 swooped down, opposed only by the unpractised anti-aircraft gunners, to put a dozen or more torpedoes into her and reduce her super-structure to a tangle of twisted metal. At 1423 she sank, together with the light cruiser *Yahagi* and four destroyers of her screen.

While this was going on a Kamikaze at last managed to run the gauntlet of the swarms of Hellcats over the carriers and of the massed gunfire of the American battleships and cruisers to dive on to the flight deck of the *Hancock* causing about 800 casualties and putting her out of action.

Further kikusui followed at intervals of a few days. By their very nature their losses were on a scale unacceptable in any other form of warfare. The radar pickets and landing ships took the brunt of the attacks, suffering heavily; but carriers took their share, Marc Mitscher being twice forced to shift his flag when first his flagship *Bunker Hill* and then the *Enterprise* to which he had moved were each hit and put out of action. Spruance's battleship flagship *New Mexico* was likewise badly damaged. In the British Task Force, the *Formidable*, which had relieved the *Illustrious*, was crashed on the flight deck, the Kamikaze's bomb killing or wounding fifty-five men, starting a fierce blaze amongst parked aircraft. Even the armoured flight deck was holed and dented. Nevertheless six hours later the *Formidable* was operational. The *Indomitable* was hit by a Kamikaze who bounced over the side before his bomb exploded. The *Formidable* was again hit eight days after the first but was again quickly brought back into action. Finally the *Victorious* was also hit; her armoured deck was holed but prevented really serious damage. Thus, but for their armour, the entire British force must have been eliminated.

This period was described by Spruance as 'a continuing crisis, with the Fleet, including its auxiliaries, paying a price without precedent'. The Kamikaze, nevertheless, could not but be a wasting asset. The fury of the kikusui and their magnitude steadily lessened until, by the end of June the Japanese effort had almost exhausted itself.

On 27th May Spruance was relieved by Halsey; the 5th Fleet became once again the 3rd. Okinawa was finally secured by 1st July and on that date TF 38 sailed from Leyte Gulf to begin the last stretch of the road the Japanese had chosen for themselves when they challenged in war a country of such superior potential as the United States. From now until the end of the war it was to be the sacred soil of Japan itself which would shudder under the bombs of Allied carrier planes; it would be in their own harbors that the remaining ships of the Japanese Navy would be sunk or hammered into wrecks.

The British Pacific Fleet, now Task Force 37, dependent upon its far distant and inadequate base of Sydney, was not ready to resume operations until 16th July, when they made rendezvous with their Allies.

The carrier squadron was composed of the *Formidable, Victorious, Indefatigable* and *Implacable*, the last of which had taken the place of the *Indomitable* undergoing refit. With the experience of the Okinawa operations behind them, their operational efficiency had reached a standard which enabled them to accept Halsey's proposal that TF 37 should function as an integral Task Group of TF 38.

Deficient in speed, endurance and, in some ships, lacking suitable aircraft, the task set them was a formidable one; but they managed to hold their own and earn the commendation of Halsey. Only in the matter of replenishment were they unable to overcome the handicap of slow and less well-equipped tankers and supply ships; generous help from their Ally's huge resources solved the problem.

By the end of July strike formations from the vast Allied fleet, which included more than twenty fleet carriers and some 1,500 combat planes, were ranging over the length and breadth of Japan, meeting every day less and less opposition. Peace feelers by the Japanese Government had been answered by the Potsdam Declaration of 26th July. Tragically, its terms were rejected. On 6th August the first atomic bomb was exploded over Hiroshima followed three days later by a second one over Nagasaki. Even then, it was only the direct intervention of the Emperor to override the stubborn refusals of his ministers that led to the final acceptance of surrender, with the solitary condition that the Emperor should be allowed to continue on his throne. On 15th August 1945 all operations came at last to an end.

The aircraft carrier, in 1939 an untried feature of warfare, mistrusted not only by the more conservative types of naval officer – the majority perhaps of the more senior ranks – but by those many fanatics of air power who believed that the shore-based aeroplane had made all navies redundant, had come, in the course of the war to dominate naval operations in every theatre.

When the surrender of the Japanese armed forces was accepted on board the US battleship *Missouri* in Tokyo Bay, the US Navy had in commission or under construction twenty-six carriers of the *Essex* class and three of the 45,000 ton *Midway* class. Taking to heart the lessons learnt from the vulnerability of the former to bomb attack, the latter incorporated an armoured flight deck. In addition there were eight light carriers of the *Independence* class and a large number of escort carriers. The British had authorised an ambitious programme of carriers to follow the six *Illustrious* class. There were to be three *Gibraltar*-class ships of 45,000 tons; four *Audacious*-class of 36,800 tons; eight light carriers of the *Hermes*-class of 18,300 tons; six *Majestics* of 14,000 tons and ten *Colossus* of 13,190 tons. This programme, however, was first deferred as the course of the war called for priority in British ship yards to be given to anti-submarine ships and landing craft, and then pruned as the end of the war came in sight. None of the *Gibraltar*-class was begun and only two of the *Audacious* and four of the *Hermes*-class were laid down. All the *Majestic* and *Colossus* class were laid down but the only ships of these two classes to be completed before the end of the war were six of the latter, two of them being equipped as maintenance carriers. Of these the *Colossus, Venerable* and *Vengeance* reached the Pacific shortly before the end of the war but too late to see action against the Japanese.

Both the German and Italian Navies had come to appreciate the value of the carrier, the former bringing the *Graf Zeppelin* nearly to completion before abandoning further work on her. The latter converted the transatlantic liner *Roma* into the carrier *Aquila*, which was nearing completion at the time of the Italian surrender, only to be scuttled by her crew to prevent her falling into the hands of the Germans. Conversion of a second liner, the *Augustus* into the carrier *Sparviero* had begun but was brought to a halt by the occupation of Genoa by German troops in September 1943.

The US and British Navies had plainly plenty of 'fat to live on' for the future when the war ended. No further carriers were laid down by the British, while the US Navy, after cancelling a 1949 project for a 65,000 ton carrier which was to have been named *United States*, waited until 1952 to lay the keel of their first post-war carrier, the *Forrestal* of 60,000 tons standard displacement. Many of the US carriers were placed in reserve, those retained in service being modernised to operate the heavier and faster aircraft of the jet age and to improve speed of handling. Two light carriers were lent to the French Navy.

The British proceeded with the construction of the two *Audacious*-class ships which were to emerge in 1951 and 1955 as the *Eagle* and *Ark Royal* respectively, and with four of the *Hermes*-class, the first three of which, *Centaur*, *Albion* and *Bulwark* were completed between 1954 and 1955. The *Hermes* herself was delayed by extensive improvements and incorporation of more modern equipment until 1959.

Together with the six *Majestic*-class and ten *Colossus*-class, this made up a number far too large for Britain's straitened circumstances to support. Two of the former were therefore sold to the Royal Australian Navy; one was lent to the Royal Canadian Navy until another was completed for them. Another was sold to India. The sixth was suspended when nearing completion. Of the *Colossus*-class, one was sold to the Netherlands, one to France, one to Brazil, one to Argentina, while the two completed as maintenance ships were scrapped. This left four to serve with the Royal Navy – *Glory*, *Ocean*, *Theseus* and *Triumph*. These ships, together with the Australian carrier *Sydney* (ex-*Terrible*) provided the main Commonwealth naval contribution in the Korean War.

Although the British carrier force ceased to expand at the end of the war and subsequently dwindled and now lies under sentence of death as a result of the rocketting costs of construction and maintenance of such ships, it played a leading role in the development of carrier technique. The first jet aircraft to land on the deck of a carrier was a de Havilland Vampire which did so on the *Ocean* in December 1945. A great improvement in launching technique resulted from the British development of the steam catapult which was subsequently adopted by all other Navies operating carriers.

Similarly the British concept of constructing a landing deck angled from the existing flight deck and the invention of the mirror landing sight to aid the deck-landing pilot were universally adopted. The former, by doing away with the need for a barrier to provide a parking area for aircraft on the fore end of the flight deck, and the latter, by reducing the chance of human errors in the formerly flag-signalled system of deck-landing control, permitted the operation of the much higher performance aircraft of the jet age and greatly reduced the deck-landing accident rate.

Nevertheless it seems certain that within ten years the only fixed wing carriers as we have known them up to now will be the two moderate-sized French ships (*Clemenceau* and *Foch*) of 22,000 tons completed in 1961 and 1963 and the great carrier fleet of the US Navy. The latter, having relegated a number of its earlier light carriers and escort carriers to auxiliary functions such as aircraft transports, aircraft ferries, etc., followed the six ships of the *Forrestal*-class, completed between 1955 and 1962, with the stupendous nuclear-powered *Enterprise*, 75,700 tons standard, the largest carrier ever to be built, which cost no less than $444 million. A further but smaller ship of this type has been authorised. Meanwhile two 64,000 ton conventionally-powered carriers, the *America* and the *John F. Kennedy*, have also been added to the fleet.

The US Navy thus evidently has no doubts of the necessity for and the validity of a carrier force today. In the present war in Vietnam they are playing an important rôle. Yet in some quarters doubts have been expressed of their continuing viability in an age in which the guided or homing missile is increasingly effective against manned aircraft and the fast submarine against surface ships.

It is possible that the carrier's reign as the queen of the sea warfare will be a short one and it may already be approaching its end.

Left and right:
Devastation caused by a Kamikaze:
USS Bunker Hill turns into a tangle of
charred metal after twin explosions,
from a bomb released by a Kamikaze
pilot and from the impact of the plane
itself. Fuel oil from US planes on the
crowded flight deck added to the havoc
The British Pacific Fleet suffers from
the Kamikazes. Fire breaks out on
board a Royal Navy carrier after a
suicide plane skids off the flight deck
and explodes in the sea ; *below:*
Carrier-borne aircraft grow in size and
scope. A 17 ton bomber, capable of
350 knots, and equipped to carry the
atomic bomb, takes off from the
USS Coral Sea

Appendix

Part 1

OPPOSING FLEETS AT THE
BATTLE OF THE PHILIPPINE SEA
19-20 June 1944

United States Navy – Fifth Fleet
Commander-in-Chief, Admiral
Raymond A Spruance, *Indianapolis*

TASK FORCE 58
Commander, Vice-Admiral
M A Mitscher, *Lexington*

TASK GROUP 58.1
Rear-Admiral J J Clark

Fleet carriers	*Hornet, Yorktown*
Light fleet carriers	*Belleau Wood, Bataan*
Cruisers	*Boston, Baltimore, Canberra*
Light cruisers (AA)	*San Juan, Oakland*

14 destroyers

TASK GROUP 58.2
Rear-Admiral A E Montgomery

Fleet carriers	*Bunker Hill, Wasp*
Light fleet carriers	*Monterey, Cabot*
Light cruisers	*Santa Fe, Mobile, Biloxi*

12 destroyers

TASK GROUP 58.3
Rear-Admiral J W Reeves

Fleet carriers	*Enterprise, Lexington*
Light fleet carriers	*San Jacinto, Princeton*
Cruiser	*Indianapolis*
Light cruisers (AA)	*Reno, Montpelier, Cleveland, Birmingham*

13 destroyers

TASK FORCE 58.4
Rear-Admiral W K Harrill

Fleet carrier	*Essex*
Light fleet carriers	*Langley, Cowpens*
Light cruiser (AA)	*San Diego*
(AA)	
Light cruisers	*Vincennes, Houston, Miami*

14 destroyers

TASK GROUP 58.7
Vice-Admiral W A Lee

| Battleships | Washington, North Carolina, Iowa, New Jersey, South Dakota, Alabama, Indiana, |
| Cruisers | Wichita, Minneapolis, New Orleans, San Francisco |

13 destroyers.

Imperial Japanese Navy –
First Mobile Fleet
Commander-in-Chief, Vice-Admiral
Jisaburo Ozawa, *Taiho*

VAN FORCE
Vice-Admiral Kurita, *Atago*

Light fleet carriers	Chitose, Chiyoda, Zuiho
Battleships	Yamato, Musashi, Haruna, Kongo
Cruisers	Atago, Takao, Maya, Chokai

9 destroyers

FORCE A Vice-Admiral Ozawa, *Taiho*

Fleet carriers	Taiho, Shokaku, Zuikaku
Cruisers	Myoko, Haguro
Light cruiser	Yahagi

9 destroyers

FORCE B Rear-Admiral Joshima

Fleet carriers	Junyo, Hiyo
Light fleet carrier	Ryuho
Battleship	Nagato
Cruiser	Mogami

10 destroyers

Part 2

OPPOSING FLEETS AT THE
BATTLE OF LEYTE GULF
23-26 October, 1944

United States Navy – Third Fleet
Commander-in-Chief,
Admiral W F Halsey, Jr, *New Jersey*

TASK FORCE 38
Fast Carrier Task Force Pacific Fleet
Commander, Vice-Admiral
M A Mitscher, *Lexington*

TASK GROUP 38.1
Vice-Admiral J S McCain

Carriers	Wasp, Hornet, Hancock
Light carriers	Monterey, Cowpens
Cruisers	Chester, Salt Lake City, Pensacola
Light cruisers (AA)	Oakland, San Diego

13 destroyers

TASK GROUP 38.2
Rear-Admiral G F Bogan

Carrier	Intrepid
Light carriers	Cabot, Independence
Battleships	Iowa, New Jersey
Light cruisers	Vincennes, Biloxi, Miami

16 destroyers

TASK GROUP 38.3
Rear-Admiral F C Sherman

Carriers	Essex, Lexington
Light carriers	Langley, Princeton
Battleships	Massachusetts, South Dakota
Light cruisers	Santa Fe, Mobile, Birmingham
Light cruiser (AA)	

15 destroyers

TASK GROUP 38.4
Rear-Admiral R E Davison

Carriers	Franklin, Enterprise
Light carriers	San Jacinto, Belleau Wood
Cruisers	New Orleans, Wichita

13 destroyers

TASK FORCE 34
Heavy Striking Force:
Formed 04.30 25 October
Commander, Vice-Admiral
W A LEE, Jr,*Washington*

TASK GROUP 34.1 Battle Line:
Vice-Admiral W A Lee

Task Unit 34.1.1 (Bat. Div. 7)	Iowa, New Jersey
Task Unit 34.1.2 (Bat. Div. 8)	Massachusetts, Washington
Task Unit 34.1.3 (Bat. Div. 9)	South Dakota, Alabama

TASK GROUP 34.2 Right Flank:
Rear-Admiral F E M Whiting

Task Unit 34.2.2	*Vincennes* (flagship),
(Cru. Div. 14)	*Miami, Biloxi*
Task Units 34.2.3, 34.2.4	8 destroyers

TASK GROUP 34.3 Centre:
Rear-Admiral C T Joy

Task Unit 34.3.1	*Wichita* (flagship),
(Cru. Div. 6)	*New Orleans*
Task unit 34.3.3	4 destroyers

TASK GROUP 34.4 Left Flank:
Rear-Admiral L T Du Bose

Task Unit 34.4.2	*Santa Fe,* (flagship),
(Cru. Div. 13)	*Mobile*
Task Unit 34.4.3	6 destroyers

United States Navy – Seventh Fleet
Commander-in-Chief,
Vice-Admiral T C Kinkaid, *Wasatch*

TASK FORCE 77
Covering Force Command,
Vice-Admiral T C Kinkaid

TASK GROUP 77.2
Fire Support and Bombardment Group:
Rear-Admiral J B Oldendorf, *Louisville*
Battle Line:
Rear Admiral G L Weyler

| Battleships | *Mississippi* (flagship), *Maryland, West Virginia, Tennessee, California, Pennsylvania* |
| Destroyers | *Aulick, Cony, Sigourney, Claxton, Thorn, Welles* |

Left Flank Force
Rear-Admiral J B Oldendorf

Heavy cruisers	*Louisville* (flagship), *Portland, Minneapolis*
Light cruisers	*Denver* (flagship), *Columbia*
Destroyers	*Newcomb, Leutze, Bennion, Heywood L. Edwards, Richard P. Leary, Robinson, Albert W. Grant, Bryant, Halford*

TASK GROUP 77.3
Close Covering Group:
Rear-Admiral R S Berkley, *Phoenix*
Right Flank Force:

Light cruisers	*Phoenix* (flagship), *Boise*
Heavy cruiser	HMAS *Shropshire*
Destroyers	*Hutchins, Bache, Daly, Beale, Killen,* HMAS *Arunta*

SPECIAL ATTACK GROUP 79.11
Eastern Attack Group:

| Destroyers | *Remey, McGowan, Melvin* |

Western Attack Group:

| Destroyers | *Monssen, McDermut* |
| Patrol Destroyers | *McNair, Mertz* |

TASK GROUP 77.4 Escort-carrier Group:
Rear-Admiral T L Sprague, *Sangamon*

PANAON CARRIER GROUP 77.4.1

77.4.11 Escort	*Sangamon* (flagship), *Suwannee, Santee, Chenango, Saginaw Bay* (flagship of Rear-Admiral G R Henderson), *Petrof Bay*
77.4.13 Screen Destroyers	*McCord, Trathen, Hazelwood*
Destroyer escorts	*Richard S. Bull, Richard M. Rowell, Eversole*

SOUTHERN CARRIER GROUP 77.4.2
Rear-Admiral F B Stump

77.4.21 Escort carriers	*Catona Bay* (flagship of Rear-Admiral F B Stump), *Manila Bay*
77.4.22	*Marcus Island* (flagship of Rear-Admiral W T Sample), *Kadashan Bay, Savo Island, Omnaney Bay*
77.4.23 Screen – Destroyers	*Haggard, Franks, Hailey*
Destroyer escorts	*Richard W Suesens, Abercrombie, Leray Wilson, Walter C Wann*

NORTHERN CARRIER GROUP 77.4.3
Rear-Admiral C A F Sprague

77.4.31 Escort carriers	*Fanshaw Bay* (flagship of Rear-Admiral C A F Sprague), *St. Lo*, *White Plains*, *Kalinin Bay*
77.4.32	*Kitkun Bay* (flagship of Rear-Admiral R A Ofstie), *Gambier Bay*
77.4.33 Screen – Destroyers	*Hoel, Heerman, Johnston*
Destroyer escorts	*Dennis, John C. Butler, Raymond, Samuel B. Roberts*

Imperial Japanese Navy
Commander-in-Chief,
Vice-Admiral S Toyoda

CARRIER FORCE
Vice Admiral J Ozawa

Aircraft carrier	*Zuikaku* Fighters 52 Fighter-bombers 28
Light carriers	*Chitose* Torpedo-bombers 25 *Chiyoda* Bombers 7 Attack torpedo-aircraft 4 *Zuiho* Float reconnaissance aircraft 2
Battleship-carriers	*Hyuga, Ise*
Light cruisers	*Tama, Oyoda, Isuzu*
Destroyers	*Hatsuyuki, Wakatsuki, Akitsuki, Shimotsuki, Kuwa, Maki, Sugi, Kiri*

FORCE A Vice-Admiral T Kurita

Battleships	*Yamato, Musashi, Nagato, Kongo, Haruna*
Cruisers	*Atago, Takao, Maya, Chokai, Myoko, Haguro, Kumano, Suzuya, Chikuma, Tone*
Light cruisers	*Noshiro, Yahagi*
Destroyers	*Hayashimo, Akishimo,*

Asashimo, Kishinami, Okinami, Naganami, Hamanami, Fujinami, Shimakaze, Isokaze, Urakaze, Hamakaze, Yukikaze, Kiyoshimo, Nowake

FORCE C Vice-Admiral S Nishimuta

Battleships	*Yamashiro, Fuso*
Cruiser	*Mogami*
Destroyers	*Michishio, Yamaguro, Asagumo, Shigure*

2nd STRIKING FORCE
Vice-Admiral K Shima

Cruisers	*Nachi, Ashigara*
Light cruiser	*Abukuma*
Destroyers	*Shiranumi, Kasumi, Usho, Akebono.*

Bibliography

Sailor in the Air, Vice Admiral R Bell Davies, VC, Peter Davies Ltd
Fleet Air Arm, Lieut.Cdr. P K Kemp, Herbert Jenkins Ltd
Wings of the Morning, Ian Cameron, Hodder and Stoughton Ltd
Wings of Neptune, Donald Macintyre, Peter Davies Ltd
Taranto, Don Newton and A Cecil Hampshire, William Kimber
Two Fleets Surprised, Story of Battle of C Matapan Ronald Seth, Arthur Barker Ltd
Aircraft Carriers in Peace and War, J A Skiera (Ed), Franklin Watts Inc, NY
The Bismarck Episode, Russell Grenfell, Faber
Queen of the Flat Tops, USS Lexington at Coral Sea Battle, Stanley Johnston, Jarrolds

Day of Infamy, The Story of Pearl Harbor, William Lord, Longmans Ltd
Climax at Midway, J V Tuleja, J M Dent and Sons Ltd
Midway, The Battle That Doomed Japan, Okumiya and Fuchida, Hutchinsons Ltd
The Battle for Leyte Gulf, C Vann Woodward, Macmillan Co, NY
The Japanese at Leyte Gulf, James A Field Jnr, Princeton University Press
Zero, The Story of the Japanese Air Force, Okumiya and Hirokoshi, Cassels Ltd
Battles of The Philippine Sea, Charles A Lockwood and Hans C Adamson, Thomas Y Crowell Ltd, NY